IMPECCABLE RESEARCH

A CONCISE GUIDE TO MASTERING LEGAL RESEARCH SKILLS

■ ■ ■

By
Mark K. Osbeck
University of Michigan Law School

AMERICAN CASEBOOK SERIES®

WEST®

A Thomson Reuters business

Mat #40793151

American Casebook Series is a trademark registered in the U.S. Patent and Trademark Office.

© 2010 Thomson Reuters

    610 Opperman Drive
    St. Paul, MN 55123
    1–800–313–9378

Printed in the United States of America

ISBN: 978–0–314–20272–7

To Susan, for planting the seed.

PREFACE

Legal research is an essential part of practicing law. After all, it is through research that lawyers determine what the law is so that they can counsel clients as to their legal rights. Legal research skills are particularly important for summer associates and newer lawyers because it is these newer lawyers who undertake the lion's share of the legal research burden in most law firms and other employment settings. Therefore, if you are a law student or a beginning lawyer and you want to succeed in the practice of law, you'll need to become a skilled researcher—and quickly.

While legal research can be fun, it can also be frustrating. Sometimes you easily find precisely what you are looking for; at other times you want to tear your hair out. (Yes, there is a reason why many of us in the profession have thinning hair.) Any lawyer who has practiced law for any length of time knows what it is like to sit in the office or the law library late at night, trying desperately to find that one elusive legal authority needed to support a crucial point in an opinion letter or brief that needs to go out the next day. Or what it is like to spend hours or even days researching a complicated legal issue, only to hit a wall and feel like you're no further ahead than when you started. Experiences like this are stressful, and to some extent, they are an inevitable part of practicing law. But they can be minimized, and this book can help you minimize them.

The central premise of this book is that you need a sound *strategy* for solving your research problems if you are going to be a first-rate researcher. Searching haphazardly for authorities without any clear sense of how a research project should progress from beginning to end is not a recipe for success. The results tend to be hit or miss, and the consequences of missing can be severe. To be a successful researcher, and to minimize stress, you need to approach research assignments systematically, carefully planning each step in the process while maintaining a clear focus on your ultimate objective as you proceed with your research. This book can help you do that. It sets out a clear, universally applicable strategy that leads you step-by-step through the research process.

Of course, you don't have to be a law student or a newer lawyer to benefit from this book. Senior lawyers too can stand to dust off their research skills, particularly if they've been away from research for a while, supervising cases and developing clients. For even if you have plenty of research assistance available, there are sometimes definite advantages to doing your own research in matters of significant importance. This book can serve as a helpful reference for those times you want to take the lead yourself on a research project.

For lawyers at every level of experience, impeccable research takes careful planning, and it takes discipline. If you adopt a sound strategy for solving legal research problems and follow it faithfully, you will maximize your chances of finding research solutions in an efficient manner. You will also enjoy your research more, and you will likely have fewer opportunities to pull out your hair.

MARK K. OSBECK

January 2010

ACKNOWLEDGMENTS

Many people have contributed to my knowledge of legal research, including lawyers, academics, law librarians, and law students, and I am grateful for all of their contributions. I owe a particular debt of gratitude to my colleagues in the Legal Practice Program at the University of Michigan Law School, who have stimulated my thinking about research strategy and other legal topics in numerous conversations over the past several years.

I am grateful also to the editorial staff at West's Law School Publications for bringing this book to fruition. Ryan Pfeiffer, in particular, provided invaluable counsel in helping me work through various ideas and in helping me organize the book.

My past and present teaching assistants at the University of Michigan Law School also rendered valuable assistance by providing information on the types of research obstacles beginning lawyers are likely to face as they begin their careers. Thanks to J.J. Burns, Bethany Fox, Chris Francis, Danny Grossman, Karen Hinkle, Betsy Martinez, and Gillian Warmflash for their helpful feedback.

I would particularly like to thank Danny Grossman, my colleague Paul Falon, and Margaret Leary, Director of the Law Library at the University of Michigan Law School, for their many helpful comments on an earlier draft of the manuscript.

Finally, I with to thank my mother, Elizabeth Osbeck, for carefully proofreading the manuscript. And I wish to thank my wife, Susan, both for her loving support and encouragement during this project, and for her wise counsel.

About the Author

Mark K. Osbeck is a professor in the Legal Practice Program at the University of Michigan Law School, where he teaches legal research and other lawyering skills. He also serves as a law-firm consultant on complex commercial litigation matters. Prior to joining the faculty at Michigan, Professor Osbeck practiced law for 15 years, first in Washington, D.C., and then in Denver, Colorado, where he was a partner with a large law firm.

Summary of Contents

xi

TABLE OF CONTENTS

IMPECCABLE RESEARCH

A CONCISE GUIDE TO MASTERING
LEGAL RESEARCH SKILLS

INTRODUCTION

This book is a primer on legal research *strategy*. It presents a systematic, step-by-step approach to solving legal research problems that guides the researcher through each stage of a research project. By consistently following this approach, you can significantly improve the efficiency and accuracy of your research.

I have taught legal research to law students for a number of years, and I have practiced law even longer. Yet I am continually perplexed by the number of law students and beginning lawyers who lack a coherent strategy for solving legal research problems. While most become reasonably adept at researching within individual legal sources, such as treatises, cases and statutes, they lack a clear understanding as to the specific steps they should follow when they attempt to find answers to real-world research problems. As a result, most tend to go straight to electronic word-searches. They experiment with a variety of hastily devised searches until they stumble upon an authority that appears to be relevant. And at that point, many are unsure about what they should do next to expand and update their initial research, or how they should ultimately complete the project.

The starting point for effective legal research, therefore, is this: divest yourself of the notion that legal research involves nothing more than plugging a couple of key words into an electronic database to search for cases or other authorities. That approach may work well on Google or Yahoo when you are searching for general information, but it doesn't cut it for first-rate legal research. Electronic word-searches are a powerful tool, but they need to be employed judiciously. They are not the 'be all and end all' of legal research, and to rely on them exclusively at the expense of a more thorough and strategic approach to legal research is to do yourself and your client a serious disservice.

The purpose of this book is to help you develop a more comprehensive approach to legal research. Part I sets out a

1

systematic, 5–step strategy that guides you from the initial framing of your question(s) presented to the final organization of your research results. Part II offers additional guidance to help summer associates and newer lawyers develop their research skills in the workplace, and it discusses solutions to some common problems young lawyers are likely to encounter when they begin to practice law. And Part III provides an overview of the principal primary and secondary sources of law that you are likely to use in your research.

Part I

A FIVE–STEP STRATEGY FOR IMPECCABLE LEGAL RESEARCH

Effective legal research requires planning and discipline. It is not an efficient use of your time or your client's money to just slog through a research project without a clear understanding of the specific steps you should take to go about solving the problem. You need to know how to begin a project, how to end it, and what to do in between.

Most legal research texts focus primarily on learning how to work with the various sources of law—that is, how to find and use cases, statutes, regulations, etc. While this is certainly important, it is equally important to have a sound *strategy* to guide you through each step of your research problem.

Imagine that you are learning to play golf. It is one thing to practice your swing at the driving range, learning how to hit each of the woods and irons in your bag. It is quite another to go out on a golf course for the first time and try to negotiate your way from the tees to the holes in an efficient manner. For that you need to know not only *how* to use each club, but also *when* to use each club. You need to know, for example, when you should tee off with an iron rather than a wood, when you should hit a fairway wood rather than an iron on your second shot, and when you should use your pitching wedge rather than a 9 iron as you approach the green. You need to know a variety of more subtle things as well, such as whether you should adjust your club selection when you are hitting into the wind, whether you should try to place the ball short of a stream that intersects the fairway rather than trying to drive over it, and whether you should try to hit the ball long through a group of trees when you are in the rough, or merely plunk it back onto the fairway. In short, you need a basic *strategy* for getting the ball in the hole efficiently—something that goes beyond merely knowing how to hit each individual club. You need to know, in other words, how to play golf, not merely how to swing the clubs. And without such knowledge, even a professional-level mastery of each individual club won't make you a great golfer.

The same is true of legal research. Merely learning how to access individual sources of law to find cases, statutes, regulations, etc., will not make you a first-rate researcher. You also need to know what specific steps to take and when to take them if you are going to solve legal research problems accurately and efficiently. You need, in other words, a sound research *strategy* to guide you through the various stages of research. That is the difference between actually practicing law and merely knowing how to use library resources. And only when you master a sound research strategy will you be fully equipped to handle the types of research problems you are likely to encounter in the real-world practice of law.

Chapter 1

STEP 1: FORMULATE A RESEARCH PLAN AND GENERATE SEARCH TERMS

A. Formulating a Research Plan
B. Generating Effective Search Terms and Electronic Word–Searches
   1. Generating Search Terms
   2. Generating Electronic Word–Searches

Suppose it's your first day on a new job. A senior partner has called you and asked you to help with a research problem. Now you need to find the answer. Where do you begin? Unfortunately, for many law students and beginning lawyers, the preferred method is to start by running electronic word-searches on Westlaw or Lexis, using as search terms the first relevant words that come to mind. Then they are off to the races, busily reviewing a mass of responsive cases, most of which have little or no bearing on the actual assignment. And when they finally do find something roughly on point, they have no idea what they should do next. They may not even have a clear idea of what it is they are supposed to be looking for.

Fortunately, there is a better way. By taking a little time to think through and plan your research before you jump on the computer, you can significantly improve the quality and efficiency of your research. So before you click on your "Favorites" link to Westlaw or Lexis, you need to take a step back and complete two preliminary tasks. First, you should think about your research problem carefully and formulate a *research plan* to guide your research. And second, you should generate *search terms* and *electronic word-searches* that are strategically designed to yield answers to your research problem. Undertaking these two tasks at the beginning of your research will serve you well later on.

A.   FORMULATING A RESEARCH PLAN

The first thing you should do when you are assigned a research project is formulate a **research plan**. You need to take time to think through carefully the precise question(s) you need to answer (i.e., your **question(s) presented**), and then you need to plan out how you are going to find the answers. For a very simple project, you might just brainstorm for a few minutes and then jot down your question presented, along with the sources of law that intend to consult to find the answer. For a more complex project, your research plan might be more elaborate. You might, for example, list several secondary sources to consult and specify the order in which you plan to consult them. You might also want to specify how you intend to search for relevant primary authorities. (For more on finding primary authorities, *see* Chapter 3, section

C.) And you may want to expand your research plan by breaking down the question presented into several sub-parts, and then noting with respect to each sub-part the sources you plan to consult in researching it.

How elaborate and how formal your research plan is will depend upon the complexity of your project, your comfort level and knowledge of the subject matter, and the time constraints you face. But the important point is that you shouldn't start looking for legal authorities without first analyzing carefully: (1) the precise question(s) you are trying to answer, (2) how it differs from related questions that are not at issue, and (3) the sources you intend to consult to find the answer.

Consider, for example, the following research assignment (which is based upon a case I once tried). Suppose you have been asked to research whether the contract doctrine of *illegality* applies when a contract is *performed* in an illegal manner, even though it was not entered into for an illegal *purpose*. Specifically, your client entered into an agreement with a friend to form a partnership. The purpose of the partnership agreement was legitimate: to form a business that would install network systems. Later, however, in the course of running the business, the partners engaged in a number of illegal activities, such as bribing public officials. Now your client is suing his former partner for breach of the partnership agreement, and the former partner's defense is that the partnership agreement is void under the contract doctrine of *illegality*. (Simply stated, the doctrine of illegality holds that courts will refuse to enforce illegal contracts, e.g., a contract to kill someone, as a matter of public policy; in these instances, the contract, as a matter of law, is deemed to be void.) Your assignment is to figure out whether the defendant's illegality defense is likely to succeed, given that the agreement was entered into for a legitimate purpose, and that the illegal acts occurred only in the performance of the contract.

To solve this problem, you'll first want to formulate a research plan. Start by thinking through carefully the question presented. Generally, in formulating the question presented, you'll want to think in terms of abstract concepts, such as the relationship between the parties (e.g., a partnership), the legal issues involved (e.g., under what circumstances the illegality doctrine applies), and the relief sought (e.g., enforcement of contracts, defenses to enforcement). Your question presented should also incorporate any key facts that you think are important to the analysis. While there is no one correct way to frame a question presented, it is important that you think through exactly what it is you need to figure out (and write it down), so that you don't start researching with just a vague idea as to the question you are trying to answer. Otherwise, the answer you find may turn out to be only tangentially relevant upon closer scrutiny.

A broad way to frame the principal question presented by the illegality hypothetical would be as follows: *Under what circumstances does the illegality defense apply in an action for enforcement of an agreement?* A more precise formulation that includes the parties' relationship (i.e., as partners) might be: *Does the illegality doctrine apply when a partnership agreement was performed in an illegal manner, but the parties' purpose in entering the agreement was legitimate?* Or you might hone in even more narrowly by framing the question like this: *Does the illegality doctrine prevent a court from enforcing a partnership agreement, where the purpose for which the partnership was created was legal, but the partners later engaged in illegal acts in conducting the business affairs of the partnership?*

Once you are clear on the question(s) presented by your research, the next task in formulating a research plan is deciding what *legal sources* you want to consult, and in what order. This will depend to some extent upon your familiarity with the area of law, and it will also depend upon certain external considerations, such as your time constraints. Normally, however, you will want to start by reviewing one or more *secondary sources*, in order to get a general understanding of the problem and to give you a head start on locating primary authorities. (*See* Chapter 2, sections A, B, and D, for more on using secondary sources to start your research.) Then you will want to turn your attention to finding controlling *primary authorities* (e.g., statutes or cases), starting with the source of law that you think is most fundamental for this particular problem. (*See* Chapter 3, section B, for more on choosing among primary sources.) If you cannot find any controlling primary authorities on point, you may then want to search for some *persuasive authorities*. (For additional information on persuasive authorities, see Chapter 7, section G.)

With respect to the illegality problem discussed above, for example, my tentative plan would be as follows:

- First, I would start with a broad *secondary source* (**Step 2**), such as a contracts treatise, or perhaps an A.L.R. article, in order to learn the basic parameters of the illegality doctrine and to get some references to key authorities. (For background on the various types of secondary sources available and their uses, *see* Chapter 8.)

- Next, I would plan to look for *primary authorities* in the controlling jurisdiction (**Step 3**). Since we know from law school that contract law (outside of the area of government contracts) is primarily based upon state law rather than federal law, and upon decisional law rather than legislation, I would first look for relevant *state cases*.

- Then I would do a quick search for any relevant *state statutes*, just to make sure the legislature in the controlling jurisdiction had not altered the common-law doctrine.

- If my search for relevant cases in the controlling jurisdiction did not fully address the problem, I would then look for *persuasive cases* that were more on point.

- I might also do a more extensive search for *secondary sources* (e.g., the Restatement of Contracts) to use as persuasive authority, particularly if couldn't find a precise answer in the persuasive case law.

- Lastly, I would *expand and update* my case research (**Step 4**), before subjecting it to a *final analysis and organization* (**Step 5**).

I might alter this plan a little on the fly if, after reviewing secondary sources in **Step 2**, I learned that one of my initial assumptions was incorrect (if I learned, for example, that there is in fact a statute that governs the analysis in the controlling jurisdiction). But this initial research plan would nevertheless provide me with a solid foundation for conducting my search for authorities.

Keeping good records as you proceed with your research is also important. At a minimum, you'll want to take thorough notes to memorialize your research path (i.e., your searches and the authorities you've evaluated), and you'll want to link each authority you deem relevant to one or more point(s) in your initial outline. (For more on preparing an initial outline, *see* Chapter 3, section A.) It is also a good idea to keep hard copies of the important authorities you find. (For more on the importance of good record-keeping as you research, *see* Chapter 6, sections A and E.)

Whether it is complex or simple, formulating a research plan is important because it provides direction for your research. It clarifies your ultimate objective (i.e., the precise legal research problem you need to solve), and it provides a roadmap to help you get there.

B. GENERATING EFFECTIVE SEARCH TERMS AND ELECTRONIC WORD–SEARCHES

In addition to developing a research plan, you should also give some thought to generating effective **search terms** before you begin your actual research. And if you plan to use full-text searches on-line, you will also want to formulate some initial **electronic word-searches**. *Search terms* are individual words or terms that are used to access indexes and tables of contents for the various sources of law; *electronic word-searches* are combinations of search terms arranged in such a way that they enable full-text searches of documents. The success of your research project will hinge in no small measure on how skillfully you employ these linguistic tools.

1. Generating Search Terms

Whether you are researching on-line or in a library, you will need to start with effective *search terms* in order to efficiently and accurately locate legal authorities. These terms enable you to access indexes and tables of contents for various authorities, and they also serve as the building blocks of your electronic word-searches if you decide to run full-text searches on-line. Generally, if you've framed your question presented adequately, your principal search terms should flow naturally from it, though you may have to supplement the terms or modify them to ensure that they are not too broad or narrow.

Suppose, for example, you are trying to generate search terms to research the contract-illegality problem discussed in sub-section A of this chapter. You could start by generating some simple search terms such as "partnership," "contract," "defenses," "illegality," "enforcement," and "performed" that flow directly from the wording of the question presented. These terms would likely be sufficient to enable you to find some relevant entries in the topical index or table of contents of a particular source, such as a treatise or a digest. But they might also miss some relevant entries if you don't broaden them a bit. For one thing, you would need to consider different *variations* of the key words. You might, for example, find a discussion of illegality listed under an index heading such as *Illegal Bargains* rather than the heading *Illegality Doctrine*. Likewise, you might find a discussion of specific performance under a heading such as *Contractual Remedies* (or just *Remedies*) rather than under the heading *Contracts*. So it is important to be flexible and consider variations of your search terms, whether you are using the search terms to access indexes or to construct electronic word-searches (*see* sub-section (2) below.) It is also important to consider *synonyms* for your search terms. If, for example, you are looking at the index to a secondary source for entries under the heading *Contracts*, you'll also want to look under the heading *Agreements*. Likewise, if you are searching the index to a digest for cases concerning overdrawn checks, you'll want to look for the heading *Drafts* in addition to the heading *Checks*.

But even if you employ synonyms and properly capture word variations, your initial search terms may still prove to be too narrow if you fail to think *conceptually* about the answers you are looking for. The Restatement (Second) of Contracts, for example, does not discuss the illegality doctrine per se, but instead includes a discussion about the enforcement of contracts entered into for an illegal purpose under a more general chapter entitled *Unenforceability on Grounds of Public Policy. See* Restatement (Second) of Contracts § 178, *et seq.* (1979). You would therefore need to think more broadly about the various *categories* of contract defenses, rather than just the particular defense of illegality, in order to find the Restatement's discussion about the enforceability of illegal contracts. So if your initial search terms are not productive, it is helpful to think of broader concepts that encompass them. Instead of "checks" or "drafts," for example, try broader categories such as "commercial paper" or "negotiable instruments." Instead of "dogs" and "cats," try "house pets," or "domestic animals." Sometimes it is necessary to think creatively about how the editor might have cataloged a topic and to try some different possibilities if you don't see what you are looking for right away.

By accessing tables of contents and indexes in this way with your basic search terms (broadening them as necessary), you should generally be able to locate authorities in most legal sources without too much difficulty, whether you are looking in print sources or on-line. Most legal sources are thoroughly indexed, so normally you can do all or most of your research without the benefit of electronic word-searches if you choose to do so.

2.   Generating Electronic Word–Searches

While using the types of individual search terms discussed in the previous section would generally enable you to access tables of contents and indexes effectively, using *electronic word-searches* to find authorities requires a little more finesse. Thus, in addition to generating individual search terms at the beginning of your project, you should also think about how you are going to *combine* these search terms into electronic word-searches, if you plan to do at least some of your research by executing full-text searches of documents. You should plan on revisiting these searches (*see* Chapter 2, section D) after you have had a chance to review secondary sources (**Step 2**), because the secondary sources will often provide you terms of art that you can use for additional search terms.

Electronic word-searches can be very helpful when used properly because they allow you to customize your search efforts. If you are having trouble finding your particular topic in a table of contents or an index, you can use an electronic word-search to scan whole texts of documents to hone in on relevant material with great precision. In the hands of a skilled researcher, electronic word-searches are often more efficient as well because they allow you to find what you are looking for very quickly.

There are basically two types of electronic word-searches that you can run on commercial services such as Westlaw and Lexis. The easier type of electronic word-search to use is a *natural-language search*, which is probably what you are familiar with from generic internet searching. With natural language searches, you just enter a question, a phrase or just a combination of search terms (e.g., "contract illegal enforcement"), and the search engine does the work for you, listing in descending order (from most responsive to least responsive) a set number of documents that are responsive to your search terms. The other type of electronic word-search is a *terms-and-connectors* search (also known as a "Boolean" search), which allows you to specify the precise relationship between the search terms you employ by using logical symbols. For example, you might run an electronic word-search like "(contract /3 illegal) /s enforce," which instructs the search engine to first find only those authorities that combine the words "contract" and "illegal" within three words of each other, and to then narrow the results to those that also contain that combination within the same sentence as the word "enforce."

When you formulate search terms for purposes of terms-and-connectors searches, it is important to capture plurals and all the other possible variations of the terms (e.g., "plums" as well as "plum," "contractual" as well as "contract," "illegal" as well as "illegality") so that your search casts a wide enough net. As discussed in Chapter 3, this is one way in which terms-and-connectors searches are less forgiving than natural-language searches. The easy way to address this on Westlaw and Lexis is to add the exclamation point symbol ["!"] to the root of a word, which enables the search to capture all possible variations of the root. For example, by using "enforc!" as a search term, you can capture all the different variations of the root, such as "enforce," "enforcement," "enforceable," and "enforcing." If you just want to capture simple, one-character variations (e.g., "men" as well as "man"), you can instead add an asterisk symbol [*] to a word, which enables the search to capture one wildcard character.

Crafting effective electronic word-searches can be challenging, particularly for terms-and-connectors searches. There is no simple algorithm for how to combine search terms and connectors into electronic word-searches, though it is helpful to think about the type of rule you are looking for with your search, and to anticipate how the courts or legislature would likely have worded the rule. Then you can use terms and connectors to frame your search so that it captures cases with that wording or related wording. With the illegality hypothetical, for example, you might anticipate finding a rule in the case law to the effect that *contracts formed for an illegal purpose are not enforceable*. To capture cases following that rule, you could frame a terms-and-connectors search such as "contract* /s "illegal purpose" /s enforce!" Formulating the search in this way would enable the search engine to find cases that track the wording of your anticipated rule. (You should be prepared to broaden your initial search as described below, however, if it does not yield as many cases on point as you anticipated.)

Ideally, of course, the goal is to formulate your electronic word-searches in such a way that you find *all* the relevant authorities that are out there and *only* those relevant authorities. Unfortunately, in the real world, that is not likely to happen very often. But you want to do your best to make your electronic word-searches *broad* enough so that you don't miss important authorities, and *narrow* enough that you don't waste a lot of time reviewing irrelevant authorities. And it is finding the proper balance between overly broad and overly narrow that makes crafting effective electronic word-searches challenging for the legal researcher.

It is generally a good idea to err on the side of broadness in your initial searches so that you don't miss important authorities; you can easily edit your search to make it narrower if the initial search turns out to be too broad. This methodology also tends to make for less-expensive searches if you are being billed on a per-search basis, since the commercial services typically don't charge you as much when you edit a search as when you run a new search. (For more on the costs associated with computer research, *see* Chapter 6, section C.)

One way to broaden electronic word-searches is to use more expansive *search terms*, as discussed in the previous section. Additionally, you can broaden the scope of your searches by using *fewer* search terms. A search like "contract illegality," for example, will normally generate more responsive hits than a search like "contract illegality purpose performance." And if you are using *terms-and-connectors* searches, you can make your searches broader by using less restrictive connectors. Replacing the connector "/3" with a broader connector such as "/15" or "/p," for example, or replacing an "and" with an "or," will cause your search to cast a wider net.

On the other hand, if you find that your research results are unmanageable because you are generating *too many* tangentially related responses, you will want to edit your searches to make them *narrower*. To do this, you should first consider whether your database is too broad. If you are running searches for Ohio cases on illegality using an *all state cases* database, for example, you'll do better with a more restrictive database containing only Ohio cases. Using more narrowly crafted search terms that track the facts of your research problem can also help you hone in on relevant authorities with greater precision. For example, if "negotiable instrument" proves to be too broad a term, try "draft" instead, if in fact that is the type of negotiable instrument that your client received from the defendant; if "chattel" yields too many results, try "engagement ring," if that is the type of chattel your client is trying to recover from his former fiancée.

Another way to narrow your electronic word-searches is to add additional search terms. With the illegality problem, for example, you may capture too many irrelevant cases if you just use a broad, natural-language word search such as "contract illegal." You can limit the search to cases that discuss the distinction between contracts formed for an illegal *purpose* and those that involve illegality in the *performance* of the contract by adding those terms to your search. Lexis and Westlaw also allow you to exclude certain superfluous terms in a natural-language search and/or make others mandatory.

If you are using terms-and-connectors searches, you can also narrow your electronic word-searches by using more restrictive *connectors*. For example, you can use an "/s" instead of a "/p," an "and" instead of an "or," and a "/5" instead of a "/10." Westlaw and Lexis also give you the option of restricting the *search field* (or *segment* as Lexis calls it), so that you can confine your search to cases arising from a particular court, to those written by a particular judge, to those decided after a particular date, etc. Setting off certain operations with brackets is another useful tool for narrowing searches. This tells the search engine to perform that operation first before executing the rest of the search. Similarly, if you are researching on Westlaw (you don't need to do this on Lexis), setting off key terms with quotation marks (e.g., "illegal contract" tells the search engine to read the terms as a phrase rather than as separate search terms).

Westlaw and Lexis both provide on-line tutorials that can help you sharpen your skills in crafting electronic-word searches. Furthermore, you can easily consult with a Westlaw or Lexis representative about your searches at any time. Both services provide ready phone and e-mail access to research attorneys who are experts in formulating electronic word-searches.

It is important to remain flexible when crafting your electronic word-searches. In spite of your best efforts, your initial searches will sometimes be too broad or too narrow. Thus, you will need to be prepared to modify them and try new terms and combinations of terms (and connectors) as you proceed with your research. Remember, few researchers are so proficient that they always, or even usually, find all and only the most relevant authorities with their initial searches. So don't be discouraged—persistence is perhaps the most important quality of an effective researcher (*see* Chapter 6, section I). But it is important to spend some time at the beginning of your research project thinking about effective search terms and how to combine them into electronic word-searches; this relatively small investment of time will pay handsome dividends as your research proceeds through the next four research steps discussed below.

Chapter 2

STEP 2: CONSULT SECONDARY SOURCES

One of the biggest mistakes law students and beginning lawyers make when researching is failing to take full advantage of **secondary sources**. (*Secondary sources* are materials such as treatises, legal encyclopedias, law-review articles, etc., that contain information and commentary *about* legal authorities, as opposed to the legal authorities themselves. For background information about the individual secondary sources mentioned in this chapter, *see* Chapter 8.) Many law students and beginning lawyers see researching secondary sources as a superfluous step that they can circumvent by going directly to primary sources via electronic word-searches. But they do so at their peril.

Now I grant that there are times when an experienced lawyer who knows a good deal about an area of law may elect to skip this step, particularly when facing a serious time constraint, or when all that is needed is a quick search for an authority to support a point of law. But skipping this step as a law student or beginning lawyer is ill advised because you generally lack adequate familiarity with the subject matter to put your research results in context. Secondary sources are a rich and valuable source of information. By making proper use of them, you lower your risk of missing important authorities, and you also increase the efficiency of your research because you are not trying to reinvent the wheel looking for information that has already been compiled.

Secondary sources are valuable in five principal ways: (1) they can provide helpful background information about a problem and place it in its proper context; (2) they can provide a head start on finding *primary authorities*; (3) they can themselves serve as *persuasive authorities*; (4) they can help you refine your initial search terms and your electronic word-searches; and (5) they can help you re-focus your thinking and get your research back on track when your initial searches are not going as planned. So you should take full advantage of secondary sources for each of these purposes: your legal research will benefit significantly if you do.

A.   USING SECONDARY SOURCES TO OBTAIN BACKGROUND INFORMATION

One of the principal uses of secondary sources is providing you with background information on a research topic at the beginning of your research. This is important because it gives you an understanding of how your research fits into a larger context, which in turn focuses your research and keeps it on track.

Suppose, for example, that you have received the following assignment. Your firm represents a client in federal court. The other side has moved for summary judgment. Your opponent's motion for summary judgment is supported by an affidavit that contains numerous allegations about what some third party witness has stated. Your supervisor wants to file a motion asking the court to strike the affidavit because it is based on inadmissible evidence and has asked you to research whether an affidavit offered in support of a motion for summary judgment in federal court can be stricken if it is based on an out-of-court statement by a third party.

Now if you know a fair amount about civil procedure and evidence, you might be able to find the answer efficiently by first reviewing Federal Rule of Evidence 56(e)(1) (which tells you, among other things, that the affidavit "must be made on personal knowledge ... [and] set out such facts as would be admissible in evidence..."), and then going straight to the controlling cases to see what they say about the admissibility of out-of-court statements. But if you are not especially conversant with the Federal Rules of Civil Procedure and the Federal Rules of Evidence, you will probably benefit from obtaining some background information on the law before you begin your search for cases interpreting Rule 56. And depending on your level of knowledge going in to the assignment, you may need more or less background information.

If you are not a litigator and you never studied evidence in law school, you may need a brief primer on the hearsay rule and its exceptions before you begin to look for primary authorities. Some out-of-court statements that look at first blush like hearsay don't actually constitute hearsay under Rule 801 of the Federal Rules of Evidence, and other statements that do constitute hearsay are nevertheless exempted from the prohibition of the hearsay rule and allowed into evidence if they meet one of the hearsay exceptions set out in Rules 803 and 804. So in order to really understand cases interpreting Rule 56(e), you need to know a little something about hearsay statements and their admissibility.

Where would you look for a background discussion on hearsay? Well, you have a number of options. You could consult one of the general legal encyclopedias: *Corpus Juris Secundum ("C.J.S.")* or *American Jurisprudence, Second Edition ("Am. Jur. 2d")*. There you could quickly locate a cursory discussion on the hearsay rule, either by perusing the general index for "Hearsay" or by examining the table of contents under the topic of "Evidence." For a more in-depth discussion, you could take a look at a treatise on evidence, such as *McCormick on Evidence*, focusing on the chapter(s) on hearsay. Alternatively, you could look under "Hearsay" in the general index to the American Law Reports ("A.L.R.'s") to see if there are any case annotations that address your specific topic. Or, if your case were set in state court rather than federal court, you could review a state practice manual; these practical guides are helpful for getting an overview of state-specific law. The important thing is not so much *which* secondary source you initially consult, but rather *that* you consult one or more in order to gain a basic understanding of the law before plunging into the cases. Whichever secondary source you choose will likely provide you cross-references to other secondary sources on point, so you can easily go from one secondary source to another to gain additional information. (For more on individual secondary sources, *see* Chapter 8.)

With respect to our hypothetical research problem on affidavit requirements, the other secondary research I would want to undertake, before I turned to cases interpreting Rule 56, would be research on the basic concepts of Rule 56 itself. Again, if you are an experienced litigator and you understand the rules of civil procedure quite well, this may not be necessary. But if you do not, then it would be helpful before you start looking for case law to gain a basic understanding of how the summary judgment procedure set out in Rule 56 works, particularly subsection (e), which deals with requirements for affidavits offered in support of or in opposition to motions for summary judgment. For this, the best choice is probably one of the classic treatises on the Federal Rules of Civil Procedure: either Wright & Miller's *Federal Practice and*

Procedure, or *Moore's Federal Practice.* These multi-volume works contain a wealth of information about the federal rules of evidence and procedure and are easy to access. They discuss the rules in numerical order, so you need merely to turn to the chapter(s) on Rule 56 of the Federal Rules of Civil Procedure and scan the relevant sections for one dealing with Rule 56(e). The information you glean from a relatively quick review of that section will focus your subsequent case research and help to keep you from getting off track on a tangential point.

The other, somewhat hidden, benefit to regularly using secondary sources to acquire background information at the beginning of your research is that, in the long run, the practice makes you a more knowledgeable lawyer. Why? Because when you try to actually learn something about the topics you are researching, instead of just finding the answers to the narrow questions you are assigned, over time you begin to weave together an understanding of the law as a whole that continues to grow the longer you practice and the more you learn about individual topics. This 'gestalt' view of the law will serve you well as you transition from a beginning lawyer who researches specific legal problems to a seasoned counselor whose sage advice clients actively seek out.

B. USING SECONDARY SOURCES TO FIND PRIMARY AUTHORITIES

Another important reason for using secondary sources is that they can refer you directly to *primary authorities*. While you are reviewing secondary sources for background information, you will often find helpful references to primary authorities, which will give you a head start on **Step 3** of your research, which is discussed in the following chapter.

Although in recent years electronic word-searches have tended to push secondary sources and digests into the background as tools for finding primary authorities, secondary sources are still be helpful in this regard, especially since certain secondary sources, such as treatises, loose-leaf services, and bar journals, will identify for you the authorities that are most significant on a given topic within a given jurisdiction.

With respect to the summary judgment problem discussed above, for example, a treatise such as Wright & Miller's *Federal Practice & Procedure* not only provides helpful background information and frames the legal context of Rule 56(e), it also points you to key cases that interpret Rule 56(e), including those that deal specifically with affidavits containing hearsay statements. Section 2738 (found in volume 10B of the treatise), which is entitled *Affidavits in Support of or in Opposition to Summary Judgment*, provides a helpful discussion of the requirements for affidavits submitted in connection with motions for summary judgment, along with footnotes that contain citations to representative cases. Plus, in footnote 17 of this section, there are numerous citations to cases discussing the propriety of affidavits that contain hearsay statements, drawn from a variety of jurisdictions. So whatever jurisdiction your problem is set in, there is a decent chance you will find a case on point in that jurisdiction. And even if you do not, you can easily use West's *Key Number System* (*see* Chapter 4, section B) to find similar cases in the controlling jurisdiction.

Make sure if you are researching in print versions of secondary sources that you check the pocket parts and supplements for the latest commentary and cases. Commercial on-line services such as Westlaw and Lexis will continually update their databases, but print sources rely on pocket parts and supplements to keep current. In fact, for some secondary sources, such as the Restatements, the number of supplemental volumes far exceeds the number of original volumes because the cascade of judicial opinions keeps filling more and more supplemental volumes.

C. USING SECONDARY SOURCES AS PERSUASIVE AUTHORITIES

In addition to helping you find primary authorities, secondary sources can themselves serve as *persuasive authorities* in certain situations. Occasionally, when you are researching an issue of law in a jurisdiction whose law is unsettled in that area, you may want to cite a secondary source as persuasive authority to convince the court that your position is the more reasonable or more widely accepted position.

Suppose, for example, that the summary judgment assignment discussed above concerned a lawsuit in state court rather than federal court, and that the decisional law of the controlling state regarding the requirements for affidavits offered in support of motions for summary judgment was rather sparse. Assuming the state's civil procedural rules were roughly comparable to the Federal Rules of Civil Procedure, as they are in most states, you might want to cite to § 2738 of Wright & Miller's *Federal Practice & Procedure* as persuasive authority for your argument that the court should strike your opponent's affidavit under Rule 56(e) because the affidavit is based on inadmissible hearsay. In the absence of any controlling state law on point, this well-respected treatise provides guidance to the court as to the interpretation other courts have given Rule 56(e), and as to the policy rationale for that interpretation.

Now knowing just how to use secondary sources as persuasive authority can be a little tricky. For starters, not all secondary sources have equal weight for this purpose. An A.L.R. annotation, for example, will generally have little persuasive force, as it is primarily a compilation of case abstracts without independent analysis. Likewise, legal encyclopedias have little persuasive force. On the other hand, a respected, multi-volume treatise such as *Federal Practice & Procedure*, or one of the Restatements, if you are dealing with an area governed primarily by decisional law, can be quite persuasive. It is not uncommon for courts to cite these types of secondary sources in their opinions, either as evidence of a majority rule, or in support of an argument that a certain position is more reasonable. Other types of secondary authorities, such as law-review articles and practice manuals, fall somewhere in-between. While courts seem to cite to law-review articles for authority less frequently than they once did, perhaps because these articles as a group have become somewhat less practical over the years, a good law-review article that is precisely on point can still have significant persuasive force. For articles as well as treatises, considerations such as the reputation of the author(s) and whether the work is recent (or recently updated) will greatly affect its persuasive force.

You should be careful not to over-use secondary sources as persuasive authorities. It makes little sense to cite a secondary source in support of an argument if you have a controlling primary authority on point. And even if there are no controlling primary authorities on point, citing a case from another jurisdiction is often more persuasive than citing a secondary source, particularly if the foreign case is factually on par with your case. Generally, therefore, you want to make conservative use of secondary sources as persuasive authorities, though in the right circumstances they can be quite helpful for this purpose. (For more on using persuasive authorities effectively, *see* Chapter 7, section G.)

D. USING SECONDARY SOURCES TO REFINE YOUR SEARCH TERMS

An additional reason to review secondary sources before you begin an independent search for primary authorities is to refine your search terms, which can also improve your electronic word-searches. You should pay particular attention to the *terminology* the secondary sources use when they discuss the applicable topic; you can frequently glean from them important terms of art that will be useful in focusing your subsequent searches.

Suppose, once again, that you are researching the admissibility of affidavits that rely on out-of-court, third-party statements. You will likely learn from your review of secondary sources that a major test for whether an affidavit is admissible is whether the information it relies on would be **admissible at trial**. In the case of an out-of-court declaration, this determination largely turns on whether the statement constitutes a **hearsay statement**, and if so, whether the statement comes within one of the **hearsay exceptions** set out in **Rules 803 and 804**. Under **Rule 801**, whether it constitutes hearsay depends on whether it is being used to prove the **truth of the matter asserted**. By going back to secondary sources and paying close attention to the particular terminology they use, you can often pick up certain key search terms that you might not otherwise have thought of, such as those set off above in boldface, that would likely make your searches more effective.

Or suppose you are researching Florida law on the meaning of the *intent* element under the tort doctrine of *intentional infliction of emotional distress*. By reviewing a state practice manual or state encyclopedia for Florida, you would probably learn right away that an alternative name for intentional infliction of emotional distress in Florida is the tort of *outrage*. By including that term in your searches as a synonym for *intentional infliction of emotional distress*, you would lessen your chance of missing important authorities on point. But you probably wouldn't know to include **outrage** as a search term if you hadn't reviewed one or more secondary sources.

Thus, in addition to providing background information and direct references to relevant authorities, a review of appropriate secondary sources may sharpen your search terms, thereby making it easier for you to find primary authorities when you move on to **Step 3** of your research.

E.   USING SECONDARY SOURCES TO REFOCUS YOUR RESEARCH

Finally, secondary sources can serve as helpful tools for keeping your research focused after you've begun your search for primary authorities. At times, your initial research will be unproductive, or it will take unexpected turns that leave you feeling less sure about the issue you are researching than you were before you started. In such circumstances, consulting appropriate secondary sources can help to get you back on track and re-orient your research. (For more tips on how to re-focus your research when you are feeling confused, *see* Chapter 7, section F.)

Remember that your research plan is not a static document: it is merely a prototype that you will likely need to modify as you proceed. You cannot always anticipate how your initial searches are going to play out, so you have to be flexible and be prepared to modify your game plan as you go. You may discover after you complete your initial research that the problem is a little different from what you first envisioned, or that your initial assumptions about the law were not quite correct. Or your initial searches may simply turn out to be unproductive. In these circumstances, reviewing a good secondary source can clarify your understanding of the legal context and help you re-formulate your question presented before you proceed further down the wrong path.

Suppose, for example, that your initial search for primary authorities on the requirements for summary-judgment affidavits hit a wall because you didn't adequately review a secondary source on the rules of evidence before you began your search for primary authorities; instead you relied on the overly simplified assumption that affidavits may not be based on hearsay. Then you found some cases holding that an affidavit may rely on hearsay, as long as the hearsay statement in question falls within one of the hearsay exceptions set out in F.R.E. 803 and 804. At that point, you should go back to a secondary source, such as *McCormick on Evidence*, to brush up on the exceptions to the hearsay rule, so that you can better evaluate whether the affidavit you are concerned with contains admissible evidence.

The commercial on-line services make it easy to go back and forth from primary authorities to secondary sources after you have begun your initial search for primary authorities. Westlaw, for example, has a service called *ResultsPlus* (or *RegulationsPlus*, for regulatory research) that is quite helpful. It uses your search terms to automatically find secondary sources and other useful materials on point every time you do a search for primary authorities, and it lists these references in the left-hand column of the page. Lexis has a similar functionality; its *Practitioner's Toolbox* feature provides a list of secondary sources in the right-hand column for federal statutes and most state statutes, and its *Related Content* feature provides links to relevant secondary sources in the left-hand column when you pull up a case. Thus, if you are researching on Westlaw or Lexis and your search for primary authorities is getting off track, you can try clicking on the links to the secondary sources that are automatically generated to see if one of these addresses your issue. You can also look within a particular secondary source for references to other secondary sources that might be helpful.

Remember, legal research sometimes takes unexpected turns, so you should not lose heart merely because your initial research plan did not take you directly to the answer you were seeking. Legal research is difficult, and it requires patience. Trial and error are simply part of the process. But consulting secondary sources, both in the early stages of your research and again later in your research if things don't go quite as planned, can make the process proceed more smoothly.

Chapter 3

STEP 3: CONDUCT YOUR SEARCH FOR PRIMARY AUTHORITIES

Once you have taken the preliminary steps set out in the previous two chapters of the book, you are ready to look for primary authorities, using the search terms and electronic word-searches you generated in **Step 1** and refined in **Step 2**. Generally you will want to prepare an initial outline of the major issues before you begin your search for primary authorities. Next you need to decide which primary sources to look at for each issue, and lastly you will need to find relevant authorities within those sources. Each of these steps is discussed in turn below.

A.   PREPARING YOUR INITIAL OUTLINE

Following your review of secondary sources, you should have a pretty good understanding of the major issues that are raised by your research problem. At that point it is helpful—after analyzing the issues carefully and considering just how they relate to one another—to prepare an **initial outline** that sets out each individual issue and sub-issue you believe you will need to research in order to answer the question presented. (This doesn't necessarily have to be a strict linear outline. If you find it easier to use an alternative method of organizing information, feel free to use that.) As you research each of these issues, you should make notations under each point of the outline to indicate which cases or other authorities address that point. In this way, you "link" your research results to your outline as you proceed with your research.

Suppose, for example, that you have been asked to research the preclusive effect of an earlier court decision on a potential litigation matter under the doctrine of *res judicata* (i.e., claim preclusion). Specifically, your client wants to bring a quiet-title action to establish ownership of a certain piece of land. In an earlier bankruptcy adversary proceeding, the court determined that your client was *not* the owner of the property. Your supervisor wants you to figure out whether the earlier decision has *res judicata* effect, i.e., whether it precludes your client from bringing the quiet-title action. Your review of secondary sources indicates that there are four requirements in the controlling jurisdiction for *res judicata*: (1) the parties to the two actions must be the same or in privity, (2) the claims in the two actions must be the same, (3) the subject matter of the two actions must be the same, and (4) there must have been a final judgment in the earlier action. Thus, you will need to evaluate whether each of these four requirements is met in order to answer your question presented (i.e., whether the earlier decision precludes the quiet-title action).

Before you begin your search for primary authorities, you should sketch an initial outline, making the four requirements the major points of your outline. Then, as you find each new case on point, you should "link" it to one or more of these four major points in your outline. If additional issues arise in the course of your research, or you find that there are sub-issues that need to be addressed under a particular point, you should modify your outline accordingly. As the name suggests, your initial outline is not a static document. Sometimes the law will turn out to be a little bit different from what you expected, and you will have to modify your outline to conform to unexpected research results. As discussed in Chapter 5, your ultimate goal is to have, at the end of your research project, a detailed outline (or similar organizational tool) of all the important issues and sub-issues, linking each point of the outline with the authorities that address that point. Thus, the initial outline you prepare in **Step 3** is essentially a prototype for the final outline you produce in **Step 5**, and that outline in turn provides the framework for your final work product.

B.   CHOOSING AND PRIORITIZING AMONG PRIMARY SOURCES

After you have prepared an initial outline of the major issues, you need to decide which primary sources to research in order to find controlling primary authorities on each issue. Your *research plan* and your review of *secondary sources* should guide you in this determination. Part of developing a research plan, as discussed in Chapter 1, section A, is using your initial understanding of the project and your background knowledge of the law to formulate a strategy for finding legal authorities. Your subsequent review of relevant secondary sources should provide you with additional information about the subject matter and the types of primary authorities that are likely to control the analysis. You should accordingly revise your research plan after reviewing secondary sources if, as is sometimes the case, the law appears to be different from what you initially anticipated.

At that point, you should have a pretty good idea of the types of primary authorities to look for first. If you have a securities-law research problem, for example, and you know from your review of secondary sources that securities-law issues are governed by federal and state statutes and regulations, you would probably begin your search for primary authorities with the U.S. Code or the appropriate state statutory code. If you have a personal injury case involving negligence, on the other hand, you would probably begin your search for primary authorities by looking for cases (using a state digest or an electronic word-search) from the controlling state, since you know that negligence actions are primarily governed by decisional law at the state level. And if you have a zoning issue, your review of secondary sources would likely indicate that local law is controlling, so you would want to begin your search for primary authorities with the relevant municipal code.

Don't worry too much about making a mistake in selecting the appropriate primary source to look at first. It's not the end of the world if you begin a research problem dealing with securities regulation by looking first at case law, and then you go back to look at the relevant statutory scheme once you see that it is cited in the cases. There are more ways than one to go about legal research, and as long as you are diligent, you will probably reach the right result eventually, even if you don't start out in the best place. The various sources of law provide lots of cross-references to other sources, so no matter where you start out, you can end up in the right place. Still, if you want to be efficient in your research, it helps to start with the main controlling authority and then expand your research from there, as discussed in Chapter 4, rather than having to work backward to the main authority. Progressing logically like this instead of in a haphazard manner makes it a lot easier to stay on track and avoid confusion and irrelevant tangents.

C. RESEARCHING PRIMARY AUTHORITIES WITHIN THE PRIMARY SOURCES

After you have determined which sources of primary authority are likely to control your analysis, you are ready to search for relevant primary authorities within those sources. This chapter discusses how to do that efficiently. (For background information about the individual primary sources themselves, *see* Chapter 9.)

1. Statutory Research

Many research problems revolve around statutory interpretation. If Congress or a state legislature has decided to enact legislation in a particular area of law, then, assuming it is constitutional, the resulting statutory scheme becomes the controlling primary authority within that area of law. While other primary authorities, such as cases and regulations, may have a bearing on how the statute is implemented, interpreted, or applied, they assume a role subordinate to the relevant statute. Thus, if your background knowledge and your review of secondary sources lead you to conclude that the area of law you are researching is or may be controlled by legislation, you will want to start by finding the relevant statute(s).

Secondary sources are a good place to start in determining whether a statute affects an area of law. A good secondary source will tell you whether there is legislation on point in a particular jurisdiction, and if so, it will normally discuss the effect of the legislation and the interpretations courts have given it. Among secondary sources, loose-leaf services and specialized practice manuals are particularly helpful for researching complex statutory and regulatory issues. (For more on loose-leaf services, *see* Chapter 6, section F, and Chapter 8, section F; for more on specialized practice manuals, *see* Chapter 8, section B.)

If you do not find a statutory reference through your review of secondary sources, you can search the topical index to a particular jurisdiction's statutory code to see if there are any statutes relevant to the subject matter of your research. Or, if you are researching on Westlaw or Lexis, you can run an electronic word-search in the jurisdiction's statutory database to find statutes by topic. In both cases, you should use the search terms and the electronic word-searches you generated under **Step 1** to conduct your searches (*see* Chapter 1, section B). Remember that if you are researching statutes in print, you will need to look at the appropriate pocket parts and supplements to find newer cases that interpret the statute and to see if there are any recent modifications to the statutory language.

Once you find a statute that addresses your issue, you will need to *expand* your research to see whether there are any other statutes in the code that might affect your analysis as well. You will also want to *update* your research to make sure that the statute you found is still valid and that the statutory language has not been modified. (For a detailed discussion on expanding and updating statutory research, *see* Chapter 9, section B.)

Next you will next want to see whether there are any other primary authorities that shed light on the statute. Generally you will want to start by determining whether there are any *administrative regulations* implementing the statute. If you use the annotated version of the statute, you should find references to any implementing regulations in the editorial notes at the end of the statutory section, and also in the case annotations. And if you are researching on Westlaw or Lexis, they will automatically provide links to implementing regulations when you pull up the statute. You can also search for any implementing regulations by looking up the statute in the *finding tables* that accompany the index to the applicable regulatory code.

If there are any implementing regulations for the statute, and if they pertain to your research problem, you will next need to expand and update your regulatory research, just as you did for your statutory research. (*See* Chapter 9, section C, for a detailed discussion on updating and expanding regulatory research.)

After you have reviewed and analyzed any administrative regulations relevant to your research problem, you should then search for any *cases* interpreting the relevant statutory language. The easiest way to do this is by reviewing the case annotations in the controlling jurisdiction's annotated code. These annotations are arranged by topic for each statutory section, so you can easily see how the courts have interpreted various provisions in the statute. (If you are researching on Westlaw or Lexis, the services automatically generate annotations of the interpretive cases for all federal and most state statutes.) You can then supplement the annotations by using a *citator* (*see* Chapter 8, section G(2)) to see whether there are any other cases that reference the statute. Of course, the disadvantage of a citator versus an annotated code is that it provides only *citations* to cases rather than *annotations*. But citators do provide the latest information on statutes, so you can see whether there have been any very recent cases or amendments to the statute that have not yet made it into the annotated code. You can also find cases interpreting the statute by running an electronic word-search on Westlaw or Lexis, using the statutory citation as one of your search terms.

Once you have found case law in the controlling jurisdiction that is on point, you can move on to **Step 4** (*see* Chapter 4) to expand and update your case-law research. If you have not found any controlling cases that answer your question, then you will want to reassess your situation before moving on to **Step 4**. You may want to back up and do some additional research using *secondary sources* (e.g., a loose-leaf service) to gain a better understanding of the legal framework governing your problem. If you still come up empty after that, you'll need to decide whether to look for *persuasive authority* to shed light on the relevant statute, or whether the plain meaning of the statute is sufficient to answer your question(s) presented. (For more on using persuasive authorities, *see* Chapter 7, section G.) You should make sure that you discuss with your supervisor how to proceed in this situation.

If your problem is controlled by a *federal* statute and you can't find any controlling cases on point, you would normally want to look for persuasive cases from the other federal courts of appeals and from the federal district courts. These decisions will likely be given significant weight by the reviewing court, particularly if their facts are closely on par with your research problem. Similarly, if your research revolves around a *state* statute and there are no relevant cases from that state interpreting it, then you may want to look to cases from other jurisdictions that interpret similar statutory provisions for persuasive authority. This is particularly helpful if the controlling state statute tracks a federal statute, in which event you can look to federal cases for guidance, or if the controlling statute is based on a model code, in which you can look to cases from other states that have adopted the model code. But you will need to make sure that the language of the statutes in question is sufficiently similar, or cases from other jurisdictions will have little persuasive force.

In addition to persuasive case law, you may want to look at a statute's *legislative history* to shed light on its meaning in the absence of any controlling interpretive cases. This can be complicated, and some judges (e.g., Justice Scalia) frown on its use as an interpretive aid. But in the right case, legislative history can be a helpful tool for getting at the legislature's intent in drafting a statute. (*See* Chapter 9, section D for a discussion of when and how to make use of legislative history for this purpose.)

Another interpretive technique that can be useful is examining how courts in the controlling jurisdiction have interpreted similar language contained in other statutes in the same code. Suppose, for example, that your client's 15–year–old son was ticketed for driving a moped under a certain state statute that prohibits minors below the age of 16 from operating motor vehicles on public streets. Suppose also that there are no cases interpreting the term "motor vehicles" within the meaning of that statute, and that the term is not expressly defined, either in the controlling statute or elsewhere in the code. (If the term *were* defined elsewhere in the code, you could use that definition as persuasive authority for interpreting the same term in the controlling statute. *See* Chapter 7, section G(2).) In that scenario, you may want to research how courts have interpreted the term "motor vehicles" as it appears in other statutory provisions in the code. Perhaps there is a statute that prohibits operating motor vehicles while intoxicated, and there is a case holding that mopeds are not "motor vehicles" for purposes of that statute. That case would make a helpful persuasive authority that you could use to argue that your client's son did not violate the law concerning the operation of motor vehicles by minors.

There are other persuasive authorities that can be useful for statutory interpretation as well. *Attorney General opinions,* for example, can be helpful in interpreting statutory language. While not controlling, they give you a good idea of how a statute is likely to be enforced. Occasionally you may also want to turn to a respected *secondary authority* to help construe the statutory language. (*See* Chapter 2, section C, for more on using secondary sources as persuasive authorities.) Again, however, you should discuss the issue with your supervisor before going too far down the path of persuasive authority.

Lastly, keep in mind that on occasion you will need to research the meaning of a statute not as it reads in its current form, but rather as it existed at an earlier time. Suppose, for example, that your client, a chemical manufacturer, disposed of some toxic waste 5 years ago, but it was not uncovered until recently, and now the state attorney general wants to pursue your client for fines under a state statute that was amended last year. In order to access your client's liability, you will probably need to research the language of the statute as it stood at the time of your client's actions, not as it currently stands. This will require you to look at an earlier version of the state code, as well as at case law interpreting that earlier language.

You can determine what language in a code was amended at a given time by examining the editorial notes at the end of a given statutory section. In order to find the earlier version of that section (assuming it is not re-printed in the current version), you can check with your reference librarian to see whether your library keeps superseded volumes of codes, either in book form or on microfiche. Or you can look at the historical codes listed on Westlaw's or Lexis's statutory databases; these archive earlier versions of the U.S. Code and individual state codes going back approximately 20 years. You can also use the government's free *GPO Access* website (www.gpoaccess.gov), which retains earlier editions of the U.S. Code back to 1996. Remember that when you look for cases interpreting the earlier statutory language, you will want to focus on cases that have interpreted the language as it was at the relevant time, not as it is in its current form, which means you probably won't be relying on the most recent cases for guidance in interpreting the statutory language.

2. Regulatory Research

Administrative law tends to be quite specialized, particularly at the federal level. Because the various administrative codes are very detailed, most practitioners who make administrative law a major part of their practice tend to focus on the rules of a particular agency. Nevertheless, the general researcher may be called upon to analyze regulations from time to time. So it is important that you become familiar with administrative research, even if you do not specialize in administrative law. (For some additional background on administrative regulations, *see* Chapter 9, section C.)

If you are looking for regulations as part of a *statutory research problem*, there are several easy ways to determine whether there are any implementing regulations for a given statute. First, you can find the citation(s) for any implementing regulation(s) in the statutory notes that come at the end of every section of an *annotated statutory code*. Second, if you are researching a statute on Westlaw or Lexis, the services will automatically provide references to any implementing regulations (through the *ResultsPlus* feature on Westlaw and the *Practitioner's Toolbox* feature on Lexis). And third, in almost all jurisdictions the index to the applicable *administrative code* will contain finding tables that will enable you to quickly determine whether any regulations have been promulgated pursuant to a particular statute. (For more on locating administrative codes, see Chapter 9, section C.)

Sometimes, however, you won't have a citation to an enabling statute to guide your search for implementing regulations. In that event, you can search for relevant regulations in the applicable administrative code by subject matter, using a *topical index*. The official index to the federal administrative code (i.e., the *Code of Federal Regulations*, or "C.F.R.") is called the *C.F.R. Index and Finding Aids*, which is included with the other C.F.R. volumes. There is also an unofficial topical index available, called *West's Code of Federal Regulations General Index*, which is more user-friendly. (An equivalent on-line index to the C.F.R. is available on

Westlaw, called the *RegulationsPlus Index*.) As an alternative to using a topical index to find federal regulations, you can run an electronic word-search of the C.F.R. to find any regulations pertaining to your topic. This search capability is available on commercial on-line services such as Westlaw or Lexis, as well as on the federal government's free *GPO Access* website (www. gpoaccess.gov).

Once you have found regulations relevant to your research problem, you should carefully read the language of the *enabling statute* (i.e., the statute that gives the agency authority to promulgate the regulations) so that you understand the purpose of the regulations and the context in which they were enacted. Remember also that the scope of an agency's rule-making cannot legally exceed its delegated authority under the enabling statute; if it does, your client may have grounds for challenging the validity of the implementing regulations.

Next you will need to *expand* your research to see if there are any other regulations in the code that might also have a bearing on your analysis. And then you will need to *update* your research to make sure that the regulations you found are still valid and have not been modified. (*See* Chapter 9, section C, for a discussion on how to update and expand your regulatory research.)

After expanding and updating your regulatory research, you should then look to see whether there are any *cases* interpreting (or invalidating) the regulations. Case law is important in construing regulations, just as it is in construing statutes. A specialized loose-leaf service is one source that will provide annotations of important interpretive cases. And if you are looking at a regulation on Westlaw, the service will automatically generate a link to annotations under its *RegulationsPlus* feature. You can also use a *citator* to see whether there are any cases that interpret the regulation or review its validity, although citators only provide the citations to relevant cases rather than case annotations. A citator, does, however, provide the most current information as to whether a regulation has been invalidated by a reviewing court. (For more on using citators, *see* Chapter 8, section G(2).) Finally, you can run an electronic word-search on Westlaw or Lexis to search for interpretive cases, using the regulatory citation as one of your search terms.

If you do find cases on point, you can move on to **Step 4** of your research (*see* Chapter 4). If you don't, or if the regulations are central to your analysis, you may want to pursue more in-depth administrative research by looking for *administrative decisions* and other agency-specific sources (e.g. agency manuals, policy statements, and advisory letters) that can provide guidance as to the meaning and applicability of the regulations. (For more information on doing in-depth administrative research, *see* Chapter 9, section C.)

Finally, there may be times, as in the case of statutory research, where your client's situation is governed by an earlier version of a regulation rather than the current version because the relevant events took place prior to the enactment of the current version. In that event, you will need to look at an earlier version of the administrative code, as well as at case law interpreting that earlier language.

You can determine what language in a code was amended and at what time by examining the editorial notes at the end of a given regulatory section for its history. In order to find an earlier version of the C.F.R., you can use the government's free *GPO Access* website, which retains earlier editions of the C.F.R. back to 1996, or you can use Westlaw and Lexis, which both archive earlier editions of the C.F.R. back several decades. Finding an earlier version of a particular *state's* administrative code may be trickier. You can check with your reference librarian to see whether your law library keeps superseded volumes of state administrative codes, either in book form or on microfiche. Westlaw and Lexis also have limited collections of archived state administrative codes. Or you could try contacting the applicable state agency directly. Remember that when you are looking for cases interpreting older regulations, you will want to focus on cases that interpreted the language as it was at the relevant time, not as it is in its current form, which means you probably won't be relying on the most recent cases.

3. Case–Law Research

As discussed in the preceding two sections, researching cases is an important part of statutory and regulatory research. In addition, for some types of research projects, you will want to *start* your search for primary authorities with case law. Normally this will be in situations where your review of secondary sources in **Step 2** (*see* Chapter 2, section A) leads you to the conclusion that the area of law you are researching (e.g., a personal-injury action based on negligence) is controlled principally by decisional law rather than a statute, a regulation, or another primary authority.

Often, the secondary sources themselves will point you directly to controlling case law. Practice manuals are particularly helpful for this, as are A.L.R.'s and specialized loose-leaf services. (*See* Chapter 8 for more on these secondary sources.) In addition to secondary sources, there are two principal tools lawyers use to find cases by subject matter: (1) digests and (2) electronic word-searches. Even if you have found one or more relevant cases through your review of secondary sources, you will normally want to use one or both of these tools to locate additional cases on point before proceeding to **Step 4**. As always, it is better to err on the side of redundancy, if time and resources allow.

Digests were the traditional tool for finding cases by subject matter prior to the advent of the computer services. Prepared by West Publishing, they compile short abstracts of court decisions ("annotations") and organize them by topic. If you find an annotation that looks promising, you can then review the case in its full form in the appropriate case reporter.

Different digests compile case annotations for different jurisdictions. You can use the search terms you generated in **Step 1** (*see* Chapter 1, section B(1)) to access the digest's topical index (called the *Descriptive Word Index*), which will direct you to case annotations on your subject matter. Or if you already have a case on point, you can use the West *key number* in the headnote to locate other cases on that same point of law. West assigns a unique key number to many thousands of different points of law. This tool is very helpful for finding cases on the same issue across jurisdictions. Thus, if you found a case on point in a treatise, but it is not from the controlling jurisdiction, you can use the West Key Number System to see whether there are any cases on point in the controlling jurisdiction. (For more on using key numbers and digests to find cases across jurisdictions, *see* Chapter 4, section B, and Chapter 8, section G(1).)

Westlaw and Lexis don't have on-line digests *per se*, but they do have digest functionality that allows you to search for cases by topic. On Westlaw you can search by topic by clicking on the *Key Numbers* tab at the top of the page. On Lexis you can search by topic by clicking on the *Search* tab at the top of the page, and then the *by Topic or Headnote* tab underneath it. You can then choose from an alphabetical index of topics and sub-topics to find your issue. After you select a topic, you can select one or more jurisdictions to search within, and you also have the option of adding additional search terms to customize your search within the designated topic. (For more on using the digest functions for Westlaw and Lexis, *see* Chapter 8, section G(1).)

The other principal tool lawyers use to find cases is the *electronic word-search*, using a commercial service such as Lexis and Westlaw. Electronic word-searches are fast and powerful, but there are some downsides to their use as well. First, they can be expensive, though the cost varies significantly among the various providers and is generally going down over time. (For more on research costs, see Chapter 6, section C.) Second, electronic word-searches can be a little risky, particularly for the novice, because it is fairly easy to get off track. It is also easy to miss relevant authorities if you don't craft your searches carefully. When you find cases using a *digest*, you know that you are generally in the ballpark because your search has progressed logically from a more general topic to a more specific topic, and you get a feel for the area of law and how your problem relates to it. With electronic word-searches, on the other hand, your research lacks that background and context, so it is easier to go astray and get off on a tangent. Nevertheless, electronic word-searching can be more efficient than digest searching, if you can craft your searches skillfully.

Careful crafting of search terms is particularly important if you are using *terms-and-connectors* electronic word-searches (*see* Chapter 1, section B(2)). These enable very precise searches, and they are very effective if you use them properly. But their downside is that they are unforgiving. If you make even a minor error in formulating your search terms, it can render your search ineffective. So you have to craft terms-and-connectors searches carefully and be willing to modify them if they turn out to be overly broad (i.e., pulling up too many cases), or alternatively, overly narrow (resulting in few or no relevant cases). (For suggestions on how to narrow and expand electronic word-searches, *see* Chapter 1, section B(2), and Chapter 7, sections D and E.)

You should focus on answering your *question presented* when you look for case law, rather than finding every possible case that relates in any way to the issue. (*See* Chapter 6, section H, for more on focusing your research efforts on results.) Once you have found some relevant controlling authorities, be sure to analyze the facts and the holdings carefully to ensure that the cases are really responsive to your question presented. If they are, then you can proceed to **Step 4** (*see* Chapter 4) to *expand* and *update* your case-law research.

Before you move on to **Step 4** of your research, however, you should also check whether there are any *statutes* that bear on your case-law issue. (*See* section C(1) of this chapter for more on statutory research.) Normally, you would expect to see any relevant legislation referenced in the cases you reviewed, but it is still a good idea to a take quick look at the topical index to the annotated code or at an on-line statutory database to make sure that you haven't missed anything. Increasingly, legislation affects areas of law that have traditionally been left to the courts, such as tort law, and you'll definitely need to know if Congress or a state legislature has weighed in on the area of law you are researching.

If your search for controlling cases on point comes up empty, you'll first want to consider whether your searches were flawed (*see* Chapter 1, section B). You may also want to go back to one or more secondary source to make sure you understand the basic legal landscape adequately (*see* Chapter 2, section E). And if you relied exclusively on either electronic word-searches or a digest to find relevant cases, you may want to search again with the other tool. This is particularly important if you have relied on electronic word-searches alone, since your lack of search results may be due to poorly crafted searches rather than to a lack of case law. As always in legal research, redundancy is important here. (For more on what to do if you cannot find relevant authorities, *see* Chapter 7, section D.)

If you've searched for controlling cases using both a digest and electronic word-searches and you still can't find a case on point, you should consider searching for *persuasive cases* from other jurisdictions. A case that is on point from another jurisdiction can be quite persuasive in the absence of any controlling cases. You may also want to use a *secondary source* for persuasive authority if there are no persuasive *cases* on point. (For more on using persuasive authorities generally, *see* Chapter 7, section G; for more on using secondary sources as persuasive authorities, *see* Chapter 2, section C.)

4. Researching Other Types of Primary Authorities

If your review of secondary sources **(Step 2)** leads you to begin your search for primary authorities with something other than statutes, regulations or cases, you should follow the same basic procedures as you would for researching those types of authorities. First, you will need to find and analyze the language of the controlling primary authority. (For further information on finding various types of primary authorities, *see* Chapter 9.) Then you will need to *expand* and *update* your research. Expanding your research for most other types of primary authorities, such as municipal codes and court rules, is similar to expanding your research for statutes and regulations. Basically it just involves reviewing the neighboring provisions in the applicable document for relevance, and then searching the rest of the code or compilation (using a topical index, a table of contents, and perhaps also an electronic word-search) to see whether there are any other provisions on point. Updating your research for these sources means (1) seeing whether the language of the provision has changed, and (2) making sure the authority is still valid. As in the case of statutes and regulations, this process is usually automatic if you are researching on Westlaw or Lexis, as they continually update the sources they carry. On the other hand, if you are researching a source in print, you will need to verify (usually by examining the effective dates and any pocket parts or supplements) that the source you are working with is still current. You should check with the appropriate clerk's office (e.g., the court clerk if you are looking at local court rules) if you are unsure.

Next, you will want to search for any cases (starting with controlling cases) that would shed light on the meaning of the controlling language. If you find cases that interpret the primary authority, you can move on to **Step 4** to expand and update your case research (*see* Chapter 4). If you *can't* find any cases on point, then you will need to decide (and discuss with your supervisor) whether you can rely on the language of the controlling primary authority itself to resolve your research problem, or whether you should continue to search for other interpretive authorities.

Suppose, for example, that your research problem involves a federal constitutional issue. You will want to start your search for primary authorities by reviewing and analyzing the applicable provision in the United States Constitution. (I'm assuming here that you have already followed **Steps 1 and 2**; secondary sources are particularly important when it comes to constitutional research.) You should then search for cases interpreting the applicable provision, perhaps by reviewing annotations in the United States Code Annotated. You would look first for any U.S. Supreme Court cases, and then for appeals-court cases in the controlling circuit. If you find one or more controlling cases on point, you can move on to **Step 4**. If you don't, you will probably want to look for persuasive cases in other circuits and from the federal district courts. If you don't find any persuasive cases on point, then you would want to consider (and discuss with your supervisor) whether to research *historical materials* (e.g., records of the proceedings at the Constitutional Convention and records of the state-ratification debates) that might shed light on the meaning of the constitutional language. (For more on using persuasive authorities generally, *see* Chapter 7, section G; for more on constitutions and constitutional research, *see* Chapter 9, section A.)

Suppose, on the other hand, that instead of a lofty constitutional issue, your research problem involves a rather mundane local matter, such as an animal-licensing requirement. (Perhaps your client was ticketed for not displaying a valid dog tag on her schnauzer while walking him through a city park.) Most likely, after a quick review of a legal encyclopedia or other secondary source, you would decide that the matter is governed by the city's municipal code. You would then start your search for primary authorities by locating (probably on the city's website) the municipal code and analyzing the applicable provisions. In a matter of little consequence, such as the dog-license scenario, that may be all you need to do. But in a weightier matter, you would likely want to look for decisional law interpreting the relevant ordinance. It is possible that through an on-line search you could find a reported court case discussing the ordinance, though that is not likely. The more likely scenario is that any decision shedding light on the relevant ordinance is going to come from a local court or agency, and that it will be unpublished. (A few municipalities, such as New York City, publish such materials, but most do not.) So you would likely have to dig around a bit to find any relevant decisions. You might want to start with the website of the relevant municipality or agency to find the names of the appropriate records clerk; then contact that person by phone for information on how to access unpublished local decisions.

If you do find one or more unpublished local decisions on point, you probably won't be able to update them under **Step 4** because they generally are not covered by the citators. You also cannot cite them as precedents, because they do not have binding effect. Local decisions can nevertheless be helpful in seeing how an ordinance or regulation has been interpreted in the past, which can help you predict how it would be applied in the future in your client's case. If you cannot locate any relevant local decisions, then you would need to assess (and discuss with your supervisor) whether it is worth digging further for other types of interpretive documents, such as local departmental manuals or policy statements.

To research other types of primary authorities (e.g., court rules), you will want to proceed in a like manner. It is important to first analyze the language of the controlling authority. Next you will want to expand and update your research, as described above. And then you will want to look for cases that interpret the relevant language. If you find cases on point, then you can move on to **Step 4**, expanding and (if possible) updating your case research. And if you cannot locate any decisions on point, then you will need to decide (in conjunction with your supervisor) whether the clarity of the language and the importance of the project justifies digging further for other types of interpretive documents that may shed light on the meaning of the relevant language, or whether you can comfortably rely on the controlling language itself to resolve your research problem.

Chapter 4

STEP 4: EXPAND AND UPDATE YOUR CASE RESEARCH

A. Examining Your Cases for References to Earlier Cases
B. Using Key Numbers to Find Additional Cases
C. Using a Citator to Expand and Update Your Case Research
D. Expanding and Updating Your Research for Other Types of Primary Authorities

A fairly common mistake among newer lawyers is failing to fully *expand* and *update* their case research. Yet this step is essential to making sure that your research results are complete and current. So before you move on to **Step 5** to finalize your research, you should make sure that you have taken the necessary measures to ensure that you have found all the valid cases that are on point. This chapter discusses those measures.

A. EXAMINING YOUR CASES FOR REFERENCES TO EARLIER CASES

You should start by examining the cases you have already found for references to earlier cases on point. Often, you will discover that the cases you found in your initial search rely on, or at least cite, other relevant cases that you did not uncover. If these cited cases appear from the context of your citing case to be on point, then you should review them to see whether in fact they address your issue. If so, then you should consider incorporating them into your research results if they are factually on point or otherwise helpful in resolving your research problem.

Whether you should include an earlier case in your research results depends in large part on the type of case it is and how it relates to what you have already found. For example, if you have found a controlling state-supreme-court case right on point, and it cites a decision from another state, the latter case probably won't be of much help to you, unless for some reason you need a persuasive authority (*see* Chapter 7, section G for more on persuasive authorities). Similarly, if it cites an *older* supreme-court case from the controlling state, that won't generally add anything, unless the older case is closer to your problem on the facts.

On the other hand, if you have found three court-of-appeals cases from the controlling jurisdiction in your initial research, and they all rely on a supreme-court case from the same jurisdiction that you didn't find, you will definitely want to look at the supreme-court case to see whether it is germane to your research problem. Likewise, if you found three court-of-appeals cases roughly on point, but none is very close to your problem on the facts, you may want to check their citations to earlier cases to see if any of these earlier cases is closer on the facts. If so, then you would probably want to include the case(s) that is closer on the facts with your research results. (*See* Chapter 5, section A(2) for a further discussion of prioritizing your final research results.)

B. USING KEY NUMBERS TO FIND ADDITIONAL CASES

Another helpful way to expand your case research is to take advantage of West's *Key Number System.* This is an important feature of West's American Digest System that links that system to West's National Reporter System. As discussed further in Chapter 8, section G(1), West divides the law into approximately 400 major legal topics for purposes of its digest system and arranges them alphabetically. It then divides and sub-divides these topics into smaller and smaller categories that ultimately reduce to individual points of law (approximately 100,000 in all), each identified by its own "key number" (or more accurately, by its own unique topic and key number).

If you look at a case from the National Reporter System, you will see that the West editors have added *headnotes* that summarize the various legal topics discussed in the case, and next to each headnote you will see one or more key-shaped symbols with a topic and number next to it. Those are the key numbers. The most specific key number corresponds to the particular point of law discussed in the headnote. Thus, if you have found a case that is responsive to your research problem, you can use its unique key number to find other cases on that point of law, either in the same jurisdiction or in any other jurisdiction.

Suppose, for example, that you are researching Florida law regarding the privilege defense to the tort of intentional infliction of emotional distress ("IIED"), and that you have found a case in your preliminary research that is right on point: *Metropolitan Life Ins. Co. v. McCarson*, 467 So. 2d 277 (Fla. 1985). By looking at the headnotes to that case, you see that headnote No. 2 summarizes the court's holding that the defendant insurer is not liable to the plaintiff for IIED because its actions were privileged. Next to this headnote is a series of key numbers, starting on top with the broad topic "Damages" (which is assigned the key number *Damages 115*), and ending on the bottom with the sub-topic "Privilege or Immunity; Exercise of Legal Rights" (which is assigned the key number *Damages 115K57.49*). The beauty of West's Key Number System is that you can use this latter key number (*Damages 115K57.49*) to find other cases on the same point, for any or all jurisdictions, by just looking up the applicable number(s) in the appropriate digest(s).

You can access the West Key Number System on-line as well as in print, though only Westlaw has access to on-line because it is a proprietary service of West's. The on-line feature is very easy to use on Westlaw; you just click on the key number itself, then click on one or more boxes to select whatever jurisdictions you want to search. You also have the option of adding your own search terms to an on-line key-number search to customize it to your specific research problem.

While only Westlaw has access to the on-line West Key Number System *per se*, Lexis has a somewhat similar functionality that organizes points of law by headnote. Lexis has developed its own unique system of headnotes, different from those found in the West National Reporter Service. At the end of each headnote is a link entitled *More Like This Headnote*. Clicking on this link allows you to find cases discussing the same or similar point of law in whichever jurisdiction(s) you subsequently select.

One important point to remember when using key numbers (or Lexis headnotes) to expand your research is that the editors do not always catalogue cases exactly as you might think they would. So it is helpful to search for cases using several related key numbers (Westlaw lets you combine them easily by clicking the appropriate boxes) rather than just the one that looks to be on point, to ensure that you don't miss any relevant cases.

If you are expanding your Florida research on the privilege defense to IIED, for example, you might want to search under key number *Damages 115K57.19*, which is the general key number corresponding to the broader topic of IIED, as well as key number *Damages 115K57.49*, which is the more specific key number corresponding to the topic of privilege. Or you might try looking under one or more related key numbers, such as *Damages 115 K57.21*, which corresponds to the topic "Elements of IIED, generally," to capture more cases. Often you can find these related key numbers listed with your original key number in the same headnote, or you can find them in one of the other headnotes for the case. You can also find them by looking at the outline of key numbers for a particular major topic, or by looking up your topic in the Descriptive Word Index. If you are using Westlaw, you can find the key numbers for specific topics by clicking on the *Key Numbers* tab. (Click on the *Search* tab followed by the *by Topic or Headnote* tab if you want to access the digest function on Lexis.) You can then search for your topic either by using search terms or by using an outline. Remember, for purposes of expanding your research, it is better to err on the side of finding too many cases than too few, so don't hesitate to try multiple key numbers.

Getting accustomed to using the West Key Number System can take a little practice. But once you get used to it, the system is easy to use, particularly on-line. And it makes a very helpful tool for expanding your case research, especially if you have relied exclusively on electronic word-searches for your preliminary research in **Step 3**.

C. USING A CITATOR TO EXPAND AND UPDATE YOUR CASE RESEARCH

After you have expanded your research by (1) reviewing your existing cases for references to earlier cases, and (2) by using the West Key Number System (or the Lexis headnote system) to look at digest annotations on the topic, you should then use a *case citator* to find more recent authorities on point, and to make sure that your existing cases are still valid. (For more on citators, see Chapter 8, section G(2).) This is probably the most important part of **Step 4**.

Once again, the headnotes of your cases are significant here. Each headnote in a case identifies a specific point of law, and the headnotes are numbered consecutively. When you "Shepardize" a case (i.e., check it with a citator), the citator will tell you what later cases have cited the case you entered. Moreover, the citator will often indicate what specific points of law from your original case those citing cases discuss. Thus, if you found the *McCarson* case discussed above in section B as part of your research, and if headnote 2 of that case discusses the point of law that is relevant to your research problem, then you can use a citator to find later cases addressing that same point of law. Just enter the citation of *McCarson* in the citator of your choice, then click on the *Citing References* link if you are using KeyCite, or the *Shepard's for Research* box if you are using Shepard's, and look for the symbol **HN2** next to the citations listed. This tells you that the citing case not only cites *McCarson,* but that it also discusses the same point of law that was discussed in headnote [2] of *McCarson*.

By using a citator in this manner, you can find all the cases, from every jurisdiction (or you can look at a particular jurisdiction), that have cited your original cases (i.e., those you found in **Step 3**) and have discussed the same points of law. If after reviewing the cases from the controlling jurisdiction (and any others you deem potentially important) you determine that some of them are indeed responsive to your research problem, then you should Shepardize them as well to see if there are any still-later cases from the controlling jurisdiction that discuss the relevant point of law. And you should keep doing this with each new case you find that is on point until there are no more recent cases to check. At that point, you will have thoroughly updated your case research. (Note that some citing cases don't have any bracketed headnote numbers next to them, so you won't be able to tell without reading these cases what points of law they discuss. But if a case is important to your analysis, you should probably take a look at all of the citing cases from the controlling jurisdiction that are listed by the citator, just to make sure you don't miss any significant cases.)

Finally, in addition to using a citator to *update* your case research, you also need to use the citator to make sure that all cases you plan to rely on are still *valid* and have not, for example, been overruled or reversed. (*See* Chapter 8, section G(2) if you are not sure how to do this.) And if it's been a while since you validated a case, or you are not sure whether you've checked it already, check it again. It never hurts to validate all your cases again with a citator at the end of your research, as there are few worse fates for the legal researcher than turning in a work product that relies on an invalid authority. (For more on the importance of verifying the validity of your authorities, *see* Chapter 6, section J.)

D. EXPANDING AND UPDATING YOUR RESEARCH FOR OTHER TYPES OF PRIMARY AUTHORITIES

In addition to expanding and updating your *case* research, it is also necessary to expand and update your research for statutes, regulations, and other types of primary authorities to ensure that you have found all related provisions on point and that your research results are still valid. However, since there is generally less involved in expanding and updating these authorities, and since the updating process is largely automatic if you are researching on Westlaw or Lexis, I have included the expanding and updating process for statutes, regulations, and other types of primary authorities in **Step 3**, which discusses the research process generally for these sources. Thus, if you have properly followed the procedures set out in Chapter 3, your initial research should already be complete and up-to-date. (For a detailed discussion on expanding and updating your statutory and regulatory research, *see* Chapter 9, sections B and C; for a discussion on expanding and updating your research for other types of primary authorities, *see* Chapter 3, section C(4).)

Remember that in addition to expanding and updating your research for statutes, regulations, and other primary authorities, such as court rules and municipal ordinances, you will also want to look for cases (and perhaps other authorities) to interpret the meaning of the controlling language. (*See* Chapter 3, sections C(1), C(2), and C(4), for more on this topic.)

Chapter 5

STEP 5: ANALYZE AND ORGANIZE YOUR RESEARCH RESULTS

A. Analyzing Your Research Results
   1. Pruning Tangential Authorities
   2. Prioritizing and Harmonizing Cases
      (a) Prioritizing Cases
      (b) Harmonizing Cases
   3. Evaluating Your Answer
B. Organizing Your Research Results

Your last step in any research project involves thinking carefully about your research results. There are two aspects to this. First, you need to carefully *analyze* your research results. Hopefully, you have done some of this in **Steps 3 and 4**, as you decided which authorities were relevant to your research problem. But it is important before you move on to preparing your ultimate work product that you undertake a further, more detailed analysis of your research to make sure that you have garnered the best possible support for your conclusion(s), and that you have carefully evaluated how these authorities address your research problem. Second, you need to *organize* your research results, integrating them into your *final outline*. Taking the time to assess your research results in this manner will greatly facilitate a smooth transition from your research project to your ultimate work product.

A. ANALYZING YOUR RESEARCH RESULTS

There are three discreet tasks involved in analyzing your research results. First, you should endeavor to prune away those that are not really on point; second, you should give some thought to prioritizing and harmonizing those that remain; and finally, you should evaluate carefully whether your analysis of your final research results provides an appropriate answer to your question(s) presented. Each of these tasks is discussed in turn below.

1. Pruning Tangential Authorities

First, it is important to scrutinize the authorities you've found to make sure that they are really on point. Sometimes your research will lead you down pathways that end up being tangential to your question presented. And sometimes the direction of your research changes a bit as you learn more about an area of law. Furthermore, with *case law* there are often subtleties in the facts or the holdings that upon closer reading render them inapposite to your analysis. So you need to read each authority you plan to rely on carefully to make sure that it is really germane to your analysis and not just tangentially related.

At times in my legal-research-and-writing class I use a civil assault problem for one of my memo assignments. Invariably, there are students who rely heavily and unreflectively on criminal cases in their analyses of civil assault, even though the legal standards for criminal assault and civil assault are different. While criminal cases may have *some* bearing on a civil analysis, they need to be employed cautiously, and the issue should be brought to the reader's attention. Using such cases unreflectively indicates that the student has not subjected his or her research to careful analysis to ensure that it is truly responsive to the questions the memo is supposed to address. So you need to think carefully about whether there is anything about your authorities that would make them inapplicable, and in particular about whether the facts of a given case are just too different from your research scenario to make the case useful for your purposes, even if the subject matter is relevant.

2. Prioritizing and Harmonizing Cases

The next task is to *prioritize* and *harmonize* the case law you found in your research. By prioritizing cases, I mean that if you have multiple cases that stand for the same rule, you should decide which of them you want to rely on in your analysis. By harmonizing cases, I mean that you need to analyze seemingly disparate holdings and determine how they relate to each other.

(a) Prioritizing Cases

While it is sometimes helpful to cite multiple cases on an important point, you generally do not want to overwhelm the reader with a lot of lengthy string citations, as this needlessly disrupts the flow of your writing. As a rule, you should cite no more cases than you need to make your point effectively. So if you have found multiple cases on the same point, you will need to decide which one(s) to use in your analysis.

Suppose, for example, that you have a fairly recent state-supreme-court opinion on a certain point of law, and that it affirms the decisions of several earlier appeals-court decisions. There is generally no advantage to including all the citations in a string cite to support that point. The supreme-court decision alone is sufficient. (An exception would be where one of the lower-court cases is more on par factually with your case; in that scenario you might want to cite both the supreme-court decision and the most applicable appeals-court decision.) In choosing which case(s) to rely on in situations where you have found multiple cases on the same point, you should look to several factors, including the factual similarity with your research problem, which court decided the case (*see also* the discussion below regarding case hierarchy), and, to a lesser extent, the age of the case. The first factor, factual similarity, is one beginning researchers tend to under-emphasize. Law is more about stories than rules, and if you can show a court that your case is factually on par with a particular precedent, it is much more effective than just trying to apply the rule of the precedent abstractly to your own factual scenario.

(b) Harmonizing Cases

The need to *harmonize* decisions arises when you have multiple cases addressing a point of law, but they stand for different rules. In that situation you will want to evaluate how the holdings relate to each other, which will determine how you use them. One case, for example, may state a general rule, while two others on the same topic explicitly carve out exceptions to the general rule. You will need to be clear on these relationships before you prepare your final outline of your research results, which is discussed below in Section B of this chapter.

Harmonizing case law is particularly important where you have cases that appear to present *conflicting* holdings on a point of law. In that situation, you will generally want to try to harmonize the holdings by formulating a rule that gives a consistent reading to the facially disparate cases. But occasionally you may instead decide (particularly if you are writing a persuasive brief) that one case is consistent with the controlling law and the other is not. It could be, for example, that the earlier holding is now outdated and is no longer a valid authority; or it could be that one holding is from another jurisdiction, and that jurisdiction follows a different legal rule than the controlling jurisdiction. The ability to make these determinations and deal deftly with conflicting holdings is part of what sets the first-rate researcher apart from the ordinary researcher. It requires you to be skilled in *case synthesis*, and it requires you to understand the complexities of *case hierarchy*.

Case synthesis, as you will recall from your first few weeks of law school, is an intellectual endeavor whereby a lawyer attempts to reconcile and rationalize disparate holdings so that they stand for a consistent legal principle. It requires the researcher to create a new rule "synthetically" to encompass the holdings and factual backgrounds of two or more decisions. Where the holdings reach different results, case synthesis usually entails limiting one of the holdings to its specific factual context, so that it stands for an exception to a more general rule encompassed by the other holding.

Suppose, for example, that you have two precedents involving liability on the part of golfers for inadvertently hitting other golfers with errant shots. The earlier case holds that the offending golfer is *not* liable for the resulting injury because golfers assume the risk of being hit by errant golf balls as a condition of playing the game. The later case—without referencing the first case— holds that the offending golfer *is* liable because he was negligent in not calling out "fore" when the ball approached the hapless victim, who had his back turned to the offending golfer.

One way to try to reconcile these seemingly disparate holdings would be to synthesize a broad rule that golfers are liable for hitting other golfers with errant shots whenever their negligence results in personal injury. Or you could synthesize a narrower rule, such as a golfer is liable for hitting another golfer with an errant shot only if the victim golfer has his back turned and the offending golfer fails to yell "fore" or otherwise warn the victim golfer while the ball is in the air. There is no one "right" way to synthesize cases; reasonable lawyers can and do disagree in these situations as to how broadly the existing precedents should be read and what the controlling rule should be. As a result, case synthesis requires creativity on the part of the lawyer, and a sense for how a judge would be likely to apply the holdings to a new factual scenario. And it is the indefiniteness of this enterprise that contributes significantly to the intellectual challenge and creativity of practicing law.

The other principal factor that bears on harmonizing disparate case law is *case hierarchy*. Considerations of case hierarchy arise where seemingly conflicting cases have different precedential value—where for example, one case is from the supreme court of the controlling jurisdiction, and the other is a case from another jurisdiction, or from a federal court interpreting state law. In these situations, synthesizing the cases is more subtle, and in some circumstances the legal researcher needs to give consideration to simply disregarding the non-controlling case as not stating the law of the controlling jurisdiction.

Suppose, for example, that the hypothetical case finding no liability on the part of the offending golfer is a state-supreme-court case from Arkansas, which is the controlling jurisdiction. And suppose that the case finding liability based upon the failure of the offending golfer to yell "fore" is from the supreme court of Georgia. What then? Basically you have two choices. On the one hand you could simply conclude that the law of the two states is different, and in Arkansas there is no liability for injuries caused by errant golf shots. Or alternatively, you could try to reconcile the cases by reasoning that the supreme court of Arkansas would likely have reached the same result that the supreme court of Georgia did (and find liability) *if* it had been confronted with a similar factual situation. In that event, you would try to synthesize the two cases to come up with some sort of negligence exception to the general no-liability rule in Arkansas.

In a litigation matter, your choice between these options would depend upon which side of the dispute you were on. If you represented the victim golfer (i.e., the one hit by the ball), you would try to synthesize the rules by arguing for a broad negligence exception to the general no-liability rule. You would then try to distinguish the controlling Arkansas decision on its facts and argue that the negligence exception carved out by the Georgia decision should apply in this particular factual context. Conversely, if you represented the offending golfer (i.e., the one who hit the errant shot), you would argue in favor of disregarding the Georgia case, notwithstanding its factual parity with the instant case, on the grounds that Arkansas simply followed a different legal rule from that followed in Georgia. Again, there is no obviously correct interpretation in this situation; the reviewing court could reasonably go either way.

The situation is complicated further if the disparate decisions arise from different courts in the same jurisdiction. Suppose the case finding liability for the errant golf shot is from a federal district court in Arkansas, and the case finding no liability is from Arkansas' intermediate court of appeals. In that type of scenario, a reviewing court would have a stronger incentive to try to reconcile the two cases instead of simply disregarding the nonbinding federal case that carves out an exception for negligence, because courts within the same state have an interest in trying to harmonize their decisions. Even so, since the federal case finding negligence is merely persuasive authority, it remains open to the reviewing court weighing the two decisions cases to construe the federal case narrowly on its facts, so that it stands for only a very limited exception to the general no-liability rule.

A somewhat similar type of scenario is presented where two seemingly conflicting precedents—neither of which has been expressly overruled—come from the same court, but one is significantly *older* than the other. Again, a reviewing court will generally try to harmonize the cases out of respect for precedent, but it can still confine the earlier case narrowly to its facts. And occasionally courts have held that earlier precedents should no longer be followed, even if they were never expressly overruled.

These kinds of considerations are subtle and difficult, and sometimes there are no easy answers on how you should deal with conflicting cases. But is important for you to work through these issues in your final analysis in order to eliminate any waffling and confusion in your ultimate conclusion.

3. Evaluating Your Answer

Finally, after you have pruned tangential cases and then prioritized and harmonized your remaining authorities, you will need to evaluate whether you have adequately answered your question presented. Probably the best way to do this is to prepare a **short answer** to it. If you find that your research results allow you to summarize in a paragraph or two a succinct and accurate answer to the question presented, then you can be reasonably confident that you have solved your research problem. If you find that you cannot accurately answer the question presented, then that is a good indication that your research is not yet complete. Preparing a short answer is also helpful because it helps you to distill your disparate research results down to their essential points.

If after a careful analysis of your authorities you find that you cannot prepare an adequate short answer, then you will probably need to do some additional research. For starters, you may need to go back and revisit your search terms or your electronic word-searches (*see* Chapter 1, Section B) to make them more responsive to your question presented. (For guidance on how to proceed if you do this and still can't find any controlling authorities, *see* Chapter 7, section D.)

Unless you are working under a particular time or budgetary constraint, you will want to keep digging until you either find a controlling authority that answers your question presented, or until (and this doesn't happen all that often) you satisfy yourself after a thorough effort that there simply are not any controlling authorities out there. In that case, you may want to look to the law of other jurisdictions or to secondary sources as persuasive authority. (*See* Chapter 7, section G for more on persuasive authority.) You should consult with your supervisor, however, before undertaking extensive research for persuasive authorities, to ensure that your research is properly focused and to ensure that the project justifies the additional expenditure. (For more on the need to maintain communication with your supervisor as you proceed with your research, *see* Chapter 6, section B.)

In the event you cannot find even a persuasive authority on point, you should sit down with your supervisor and discuss how to proceed. Depending on the assignment and the client's needs, your supervisor may be satisfied with an inconclusive answer. But alternatively she may suggest other angles for you to consider in looking for authorities, or she may want you to use tangentially related cases creatively to make an argument by analogy. The latter possibility is likely to occur in an adversarial context, where, for example, your supervisor is preparing a brief and needs to come up with *some* kind of reasonable argument in support of the client's position, even if there are no obvious authorities on point. (*See* Chapter 6, section I, for more on the importance of persistence in legal research.)

B.   ORGANIZING YOUR RESEARCH RESULTS

The second important component of **Step 5** is *organizing* your research results. This should be relatively easy if you have followed the steps set out in Chapters 1–4 as you progressed through your research. I have suggested that you prepare an *initial outline* (or a similar organizational tool, if you prefer) of the principal issues you intend to address before you start your search for primary authorities, and that you modify this outline as necessary as you proceed with your research. I have also suggested that you take thorough notes to memorialize your research path, that you keep hard copies of the important authorities you find, and that you "link" the authorities to the various points of law in your outline. If you've done those things, then your final organization should be largely a matter of refining your working outline.

If you have a complicated research problem, you might consider using a software application to assist you with the organization, if you have access to such a tool. Several commercial applications are available; Lexis' *CaseMap* is probably the best known. These tools are particularly helpful if your research is being incorporated into a complicated brief with a lot of evidentiary support, or if it is being used for trial preparation. Applications such as CaseMap allow you to quickly retrieve for any given point of law in your outline all the legal authorities, witnesses, documents, deposition cites, paragraphs from pleadings, etc., that support or relate to that point.

For most straight-forward legal-research projects, however, a relatively simple outline should suffice, as long as the various sections of the outline include all the points and sub-points you want to discuss in your ultimate work product, along with citations to the authorities supporting each point. Once you have created this type of detailed outline, your research project is basically complete, and you can proceed to prepare your ultimate work product (e.g., a legal memorandum, a brief, or an opinion letter). The final outline, together with your revised question presented and your short answer, should form the skeleton for the first draft of your ultimate work product. You may want to reorganize your work product a bit after the first draft, but that shouldn't be too difficult once you have a complete draft of your analysis on paper.

In sum, diligently following the 5 steps outlined in Chapters 1–5 will not only ensure that your research is accurate and thorough, it will also make it significantly easier for you to prepare your ultimate work product.

Part II

REFINING YOUR LEGAL RESEARCH SKILLS

The five-step strategy discussed in Part I provides a solid foundation upon which you can develop your research skills. But merely reading the proposed strategy will not automatically turn you into a first-rate legal researcher. You also need abundant practice in putting this strategy to work. And you need to develop good work habits as you begin to practice law. This part of the book outlines some important considerations you should keep in mind as you continue to develop and refine your legal research skills in the workplace. Chapter 6 offers ten research tips to help summer associates and beginning lawyers succeed in the practice of law. And Chapter 7 addresses some common problems beginning lawyers encounter in their research, along with ways to overcome these problems.

Chapter 6

TEN TIPS FOR THE SUMMER ASSOCIATE AND THE BEGINNING LAWYER

A. Carry a Legal Pad
B. Keep the Lines of Communication Open
C. Don't Forget: Money Matters
D. Learn Your Way Around the Law Library
E. Keep Track of Where You've Been and Know Where You're Going
F. Don't Reinvent the Wheel
G. Remember That Annotations and Headnotes Are Not Cases
H. Find Answers, Not Just Authorities
I. If at First You Don't Succeed, Persist!
J. Shepardize or Perish

Learning how to do legal research in law school is one thing; applying that learning in the workplace is quite another. Expectations are different in the employment setting, and there are things you need to know that you won't learn in law school. This chapter discusses some important considerations law students and beginning lawyers should keep in mind as they make the transition from law school to the practice of law. It is based in large part on interviews I conducted with numerous lawyers from a variety of different backgrounds and levels of experience regarding their advice for beginning lawyers on legal research. You can save yourself a lot of aggravation if you take these tips to heart early in your career.

A. CARRY A LEGAL PAD

Waiting in my office for my two supervisors to come by for my first-ever annual review was, as you might expect, a bit nerve-racking. I *thought* things had gone well that first year. My supervisors had *seemed* happy enough with my work. But since I had never had a law-firm performance review previously, I wasn't quite sure what to expect. And after all, this was one of Washington, D.C.'s biggest firms, and the expectations would be high. What if they didn't think I was smart enough? What if they didn't think I knew enough about the law? What if they didn't think I was a good enough writer—or *researcher*, for that matter? What if . . . well, you know the feeling.

When my supervisors showed up smiling and laughing, the "what-ifs" went away. And indeed, to my relief, the review went quite well. Thankfully, my supervisors focused mainly on the positive, rather than my rough first-year-lawyer edges. In fact, the main thing they wanted me to work on was not my smarts, my knowledge, or my writing, but rather my *note-taking*, or more properly, my lack thereof. Specifically, one of the partners found it quite annoying that I would come by his office to receive an assignment, but I would not write down what he said during the meeting. (Apparently I erroneously thought I had a good memory for detail.) Then I would return a few days later for clarification, and still not write down what he said. Then on my third visit, he would look annoyed, pull out a legal pad, toss it in front of me, and tell me to make sure that I wrote it down this time. In the end, he was pleased with my work product, but my poor note-taking habits caused my supervisor some unnecessary irritation.

And so it is in the working world: often, it's not a young lawyer's lack of ability that causes problems, but rather a lack of attention to the little things. So take a lesson from my experience: always carry a notepad (or its equivalent) when you meet with people. Pay close attention to what your supervisor says when you receive an assignment, and make sure that you write it down. Of course, you don't want to get so caught up in note-taking that you fail to grasp the significance of what your supervisor is saying. But you also don't want to pester your supervisor later with follow-up questions about matters that were discussed in your initial meeting. Good note-taking (which means listening carefully while still recording the essence of what someone tells you) is an important skill that will serve you well throughout your career.

B. KEEP THE LINES OF COMMUNICATION OPEN

In addition to taking good notes of your meetings with a supervising attorney, you should strive to maintain good communication with your supervisor as you proceed with your research project. If you are unclear about something that is discussed during the initial meeting, ask for clarification. The best time to ask questions is while you are there in the first instance. You want to make sure that you understand the assignment fully and that you know exactly what type of work product your supervisor wants you to produce. And don't hesitate to ask the supervising attorney for more background information about the case or the transaction if you feel it would help you to understand the research assignment more fully.

Furthermore, you should return to your supervisor for guidance if your research doesn't go as planned, or if you need further information in order to find an answer to your research problem. You should also return to your supervisor if your research turns up some new leads that look promising and you think perhaps you should explore a different angle from that which you discussed with your supervisor. The important thing is to keep the lines of communication open as you proceed with your research assignment. Research can take unexpected turns, and you need to maintain a meeting of the minds with your supervisor so that you don't go off on an unhelpful tangent. This is particularly important if you cannot find controlling authorities on point and you are not sure whether to keep searching or to make do with what you have (*see* Chapter 7, section D). Your supervisor is in the best position to judge whether the extra expenditure of time and money is justified in a particular instance; in addition, your supervisor may have some helpful ideas for further research that you hadn't considered.

In the end, you need to balance the risk of annoying your supervisor with too many pesky questions against the risk that you will get off track and turn in a poor work product if you remain silent. And the latter is definitely the greater of the potential evils. In my first-year evaluation that I discussed in the previous section of this chapter, I still got a very good review, notwithstanding my poor note-taking. But I can guarantee you that my review would have been significantly less favorable had I simply guessed at what my supervisor wanted, and as a result turned in an unhelpful work product. So don't be afraid to ask your supervisor questions about your research assignment both in your initial meeting and as you proceed—just make sure to write down what she says.

C. DON'T FORGET: MONEY MATTERS

In law school, because you are not charged for your Westlaw and Lexis use, it is easy to get in the habit of relying on these commercial services freely without concern for their cost. But in the practice of law there are times, as discussed in the subsequent section of this chapter, when you will want or need to do library research instead of electronic research in order to cut costs. (*See also* Chapter 7, section B, for more on the choice between library research and on-line research.) Depending on the client, the commercial service you choose, and the nature of the project, the expense of electronic research may not be justified in a particular situation. On the other hand, while people generally think of electronic research as more expensive than library research, there are times where it is more efficient, and therefore cheaper in terms of the overall cost to the client. If, for example, you bill your client for your time it takes to trudge down the block to the closest law library to look at a case in print, instead of quickly pulling up the case using a commercial service, you are likely to cost your client money. So part of being a good researcher is developing an awareness of cost considerations and thinking about the balance of costs and efficiencies when you research.

One important aspect of this cost consciousness is an understanding that not all research projects are created equal when it comes to resource consumption. Your client's financial resources and the importance of the particular research project to the overall case will influence how much time you spend on a project and whether you should use an electronic research service. A corporation involved in bet-the-company litigation may want your firm to leave no stone unturned when it comes to a particular project, while an individual or small-business client looking for some quick advice on a relatively mundane transactional matter probably does not want you to prepare a research tome in response to its questions. Make sure you talk to your supervisor on every project to see roughly how much time your supervisor thinks you should spend on it (*see* also Chapter 7, section C), and when in doubt, verify whether you are free to use electronic research services.

I once asked a summer associate to research a relatively straight-forward issue while I was away at a trial one day, assuming it would take him only an hour or so in the library. When I came back, he had the answer and gave me a short memo summarizing his research. I thought nothing more about it until the computer-research bill showed up on the client's preliminary invoice later that month, and there I saw a computer charge for over $5000 for that one small project. Apparently the summer associate ran one fruitless search after another for most of the day before finally stumbling upon a search that worked. Since the summer associate had chosen transactional billing over hourly billing (*see* the discussion below), he was able to ring up a huge fee in a relatively short period of time for work that probably could have been done for free in the library. Needless to say, my client was not thrilled with the news, and the firm ended up eating a significant part of the charge. And I learned a valuable lesson on the need to communicate candidly with beginning lawyers as to the appropriate scope of their research and as to issues of cost.

With regard to electronic research specifically, it is helpful to have a basic familiarity with the cost of the service. First, you should be aware that different service providers charge significantly different rates. Most students coming out of law school are familiar only with the two largest providers: Westlaw and Lexis. But there are other, lesser-known services available as well, including Loislaw (which is associated with Wolters Kluwer, the parent of Aspen Publishing), VersusLaw, Casemaker (which is a collective operation of state bar associations), and Fastcase. Bloomberg Law is also introducing a new product as this book is going to publication that offers many of the same services as Westlaw and Lexis.

Some of these competitors to Westlaw and Lexis may not have all the same capabilities and coverage as Westlaw and Lexis, but their more-competitive pricing makes them attractive in certain contexts. If you are researching a complicated problem on behalf of a large, corporate client, for example, it might make sense to use Westlaw or Lexis, whereas if you are researching a relatively straightforward matter on behalf of an individual, it might be better to use one of the less-expensive services.

Google Scholar (www.scholar.google.com) can also come in handy when you are trying to cut costs. This free service offers ready access to cases and law-review articles, along with various non-legal materials. It can serve as a useful starting point for your case-law research when you are to hold down expenses. Just remember that you will need to expand and update your research after you have found some initial cases, as discussed in Chapter 4.

You should be aware that individual service providers may have alternative types of billing arrangements. Sometimes, you can choose whether you want to be charged by the transaction (e.g., by each search, or by each page you print) or by the amount of time you spend using the service. For any given project, which one you choose should depend on factors such as the number of searches you anticipate executing and the amount of time you think it will take to review the responsive materials. For example, if you plan to review a number of cases on a topic that is relatively discrete (e.g., all cases interpreting F.R.C.P. 25 arising from the United States District Court for the Northern District of Ohio), you would probably want to be billed on a transactional basis, since you could likely find everything in a single search. On the other hand, if you have a complicated research project that you don't have a good handle on and you think it may require multiple searches to find what you are looking for, you would probably want to be billed on an hourly basis.

You should also familiarize yourself with the scope of your employer's subscription service with each electronic service provider. Frequently firms will pay one set monthly amount for all the on-line research the lawyers in that firm do, but there are additional, often substantial, charges if you go outside of the firm's basic subscription plan looking for a particular source. If you don't know how your law firm is charged for on-line services, or what is covered by its basic subscription plan, be sure to ask the firm's librarian or administrator.

I once sat on my law firm's library committee, and there was a situation involving an associate who unwittingly went outside the firm's Westlaw subscription plan numerous times over a two-week period to look at sections from C.J.S., a legal encyclopedia that was not covered by the firm's plan. Each time she incurred a substantial charge, even though she could probably have done substantially the same research for no additional charge if she had used the other general legal encyclopedia, Am. Jur. 2d, since that was covered by the firm's plan (and available in the firm's library as well). Instead, the associate incurred enough additional charges on that one research project to more than pay for a complete, multi-volume set of the C.J.S. encyclopedia in hard copy.

Keep in mind also that there are sometimes free internet alternatives to fee-based electronic research services. Government agencies, courts, some law schools, and other organizations make various sources (generally primary sources rather than secondary sources) available on-line, and you can access most of them free of charge. The web sites to some of the more important organizations are listed in Chapter 9 of this book, in connection with the individual primary sources of law. Just be aware that these free resources are often not as comprehensive or up to date as fee-based services, and your ability to search within the sources may be quite limited. Still, for a cost-sensitive research project, they can be quite helpful.

Finally, in order to become more cost-conscious about your research, I would consider keeping a *time log*, with fairly detailed descriptions of your research for each research project you work on, even while you are in law school and still learning how to do research. This is a good habit to develop early on, since your employer will likely require you to keep such records once you start practicing. It also encourages efficiency because it helps you keep in the forefront of your mind how much of your time and your client's money you are spending on a given research project. While it may not be apparent in law school, money and time matter a great deal in the practice of law, particularly in private practice, and the more cost-conscious you become in law school, starting with your research habits, the better prepared you will be for the realities of legal practice.

D. LEARN YOUR WAY AROUND THE LAW LIBRARY

It may seem hard to believe, but there was a time when computer research didn't exist. In those dark days, lawyers had to rely on books alone for their legal research, which often forced them to leave the comfortable confines of their offices and trek through the office, or perhaps even to another building, to do their research in a law library, where young lawyers would while away the hours with their heads buried in treatises, reporters, and numerous Shepards' volumes. Today, of course, things are different, and lawyers do most of their research on their computers, either in their offices or in some other convenient location. So it is easy to forget the important role the library played, until quite recently, in the practice of law. And it is easy for the beginning researcher to see the library as little more than a historical relic.

Even if you are an avid devotee of electronic research, however, you should familiarize yourself with library research and develop a basic competence in using print resources as well as electronic resources. Electronic research services and the internet have revolutionized legal research, and they are invaluable tools. But there are still some good reasons why you need to know your way around a law library if you want to be a first-rate researcher.

The first reason is that law libraries are still important for finding certain legal sources. While electronic research services such as Westlaw and Lexis contain a wealth of information in their databases, they have not yet catalogued everything you will ever need to research. Some resources you still need to research in print. This includes not just obscure resources, but also some commonly used tools, such as certain specialized treatises and practice manuals (*see* Chapter 6, section F, and Chapter 8, section B) that you may come to rely on frequently if you practice in a heavily regulated area of law, such as tax or employee benefits. Additionally, you may not always have access to electronic research services. Computers and computer services can fail temporarily, and if that happens while you are in the middle of some time-sensitive research project, you had better know how to use the library. Furthermore, your particular employer may have limited access to electronic research services, or may not want you to use them on certain projects that are cost-sensitive. As discussed in the previous section of this chapter, electronic research services can be expensive, and it is not uncommon even in a large law firm for your supervisor to ask you to avoid using them on a particular project. So it is important to familiarize yourself with library research in case you need to rely on the books.

A further benefit of law libraries is that they are the domain of law librarians—and a good law librarian can be a researcher's best friend. For law students in particular, the assistance of the law school's professional library staff is an invaluable resource. If you are looking for an obscure source or you don't know where to look for a particular type of authority, a knowledgeable reference librarian can point you in the right direction. And when you are stuck in your research and don't know how to proceed, your law librarian, who has a wealth of knowledge about available resources, can often refer you to a helpful secondary source that can stimulate your thinking and get your research moving forward again. (For more tips on how to overcome confusion during a research problem, *see* Chapter 7, section F.)

One other good reason you should familiarize yourself with library research is that the printed page is sometimes easier to work with than the computer screen. For some sources, e.g., case reporters, it makes little differences whether you look at them on-line or in print. But for other types of sources—particularly those that encompass multiple volumes and contain numerous sections—reviewing the electronic versions can be a bit cumbersome. When you are researching a legislative code or a multi-volume treatise on-line, for example, you cannot readily scan the surrounding sections and jump back and forth between sections in order to put your research in context and see whether other sections are germane to your research. With a book, you can more easily flip through the various sections, the table of contents, and the general index to assure yourself that you've found everything on point. You can still do all of these things on-line, but it is often more laborious, given the present technology. So if you have ready access to a law library, you will probably find it easier to research these types of sources in printed form.

For these reasons, it would be wise for you to invest some time in learning how to become competent in print research as well as electronic research, and in knowing how to make appropriate use of the important resources law libraries offer. (For more on the choice between library and computer research, *see* Chapter 7, section B.) You should also learn what types of resources are available in your particular law library, and where they are located.

E. KEEP TRACK OF WHERE YOU'VE BEEN AND KNOW WHERE YOU'RE GOING

It is very important when you research to maintain at all times a clear understanding of where you are in the research process, so that you don't lose track of what you have already done and you don't lose sight of your ultimate goal. Think of this as the research equivalent of tracking your position with a global positioning device when you go for a hike in unfamiliar terrain.

First, you should keep good *records of your research* so that you'll know what you've already looked at as you proceed with your research, and you won't have to re-invent the wheel in the event you need to revisit an issue later. You should keep notes as to the various search terms and electronic word-searches you've employed, as well as the authorities you've analyzed, with brief notations as to why you decided to include or exclude each authority. Second, you should update your *initial outline* as you proceed, so that it reflects your evolving understanding of the legal issues involved in your research project. Your outline, moreover, should contain citations to the authorities that address each of the various points in your outline. Suppose, for example, you are researching whether your client is liable under the tort doctrine of intentional infliction of emotional distress ("IIED"), and you have a five-part outline: one section each for the four elements of IIED (intent, outrageous conduct, causation, and severe distress), and one for the privilege defense. Your outline should reflect, for each of these 5 points, which of your authorities supports or addresses that point. It is a also good idea to make hard copies of the key authorities you decide to include in your research, and to make notations on top of each one indicating which point(s) in your outline it addresses.

Detailed record-keeping may sound onerous, but it's really fairly simple when you get the hang of it. And the relatively small investment of time you make will pay off on those occasions when your research doesn't go as expected and you need to re-trace your steps—particularly if you are working on a complicated project. Good record-keeping also makes your final organization at the end of your project easier. You will already have a fairly detailed working outline that links each point in your outline to the authorities that address that issue. And you can fairly easily convert this working outline to a final outline, and then to a skeletal framework for your ultimate work product (*see* Chapter 5, section B).

In addition to keeping good records as you proceed with your research, make sure that you keep an eye on your final work product throughout your project. It's easy to get side-tracked in legal research, so you need to keep focused on your question presented and consider at every step how what you are finding relates to that question. Your outline should help in this regard. When you analyze any given authority, think about how it fits into your outline, and how ultimately it will help you find an answer to your research problem.

F. DON'T REINVENT THE WHEEL

As discussed in Chapter 2, secondary sources are important for a number of reasons. They are particularly important if you are researching in a specialized area of law, such as tax law, employee benefits, or commercial bankruptcy litigation. In these types of areas, specialized secondary materials are almost an essential part of the practice.

There are several types of specialized materials available to the practitioner. These include: (1) "loose-leaf services," published by companies such as BNA or CCH, that compile a variety of primary and secondary materials in one set of volumes; (2) multi-volume, specialized practice manuals and treatises that focus on narrow areas of law, such as federal-securities litigation or eminent domain, and (3) specialized newsletters that keep practitioners up to date on the latest developments in particular areas of the law. Some of these materials are jurisdiction-specific; others are general. Most are available on-line, normally through a subscription service. A good law library should also carry most of them. Westlaw and Lexis carry some of these specialized materials, and they also compile collections of materials organized by subject matter that may be helpful to you if you don't have ready access to other specialized materials. (*See* Chapter 8, section F, for more on specialized materials.)

The main advantage of specialized materials is that they allow you to research in a narrow area of the law without having to consult multiple sources, and without having to waste time sifting through mounds of irrelevant information. Loose-leaf services are particularly valuable for this because they collect secondary materials and various types of primary materials in one place so that you don't have to look at multiple, often obscure sources to find what you are looking for.

When I first started practicing law in Washington, D.C., I worked in my firm's health-care department, and a big part of the practice involved issues surrounding Medicare and Medicaid reimbursement. Probably the most important research tool I used (in addition to a multi-volume treatise on administrative law) was a loose-leaf service called the *CCH Medicare and Medicaid Guide*. It contained both federal and state materials pertaining to the Medicare and Medicaid programs, including statutes, regulations, court decisions, agency decisions, and agency manuals, as well as secondary material explaining the primary authorities, and updates on recent events in Congress. Looking up all of these materials separately, even assuming I could have found them all, would have been a very time-consuming task. The loose-leaf service made it easy by putting them all in one set of binders.

So if you find yourself extensively researching a specialized area of law, be sure to ask your supervisor or your local reference librarian whether there are any loose-leaf services or other specialty materials that might facilitate your research. They can make your research a lot easier.

G.   REMEMBER THAT ANNOTATIONS AND HEADNOTES ARE NOT CASES

This advice should go without saying, but my practicing-lawyer friends tell me it is still an issue for some beginning lawyers, so let's make it abundantly clear: annotations and headnotes are merely tools for finding cases, *not* case substitutes.

When I was a senior associate, my supervisor once asked me to work with a law-student intern on his writing—"it's really bad," he said. He wasn't kidding. When I looked at the (purported) memorandum the intern had turned in, I was amazed to see a 2–page document consisting almost entirely of discrete headnotes from several different cases re-printed verbatim on the paper. He even included the headnote numbers. And that was it: there was no analysis or even factual discussion, just a vague conclusion like "and so the client will win" at the end of the headnotes. Needless to say, I knew I had my work cut out for me.

Now I don't expect too many of you would turn in that kind of work product. But you may at times be tempted to rely on an annotation to provide you with a supporting citation, without actually going to the trouble of looking up the actual case and reading it. And you may at times be tempted to review only the headnotes of a case to determine whether to include it in your research results—again, without reading the text of the case itself. But you should endeavor to flee from such temptation. Annotations and headnotes should be limited to their intended use. Annotations are designed to help you make a first cut as to relevance. If there is any question whether the case is on point, you need to read the actual opinion. Headnotes are designed to help you find where in cases certain discussions are located, and to help you find related cases. You should not rely on them to accurately summarize what is contained in the actual case. Instead, you should read the actual language of the decision to determine whether the case is germane to your research problem.

Trying to shortcut your research problem by using annotations and headnotes in inappropriate ways is unwise because you risk skewing your analysis with an incorrect reading of a case. Taking the little extra time required to read the actual decision is an inexpensive way to insure against this risk.

H. FIND ANSWERS, NOT JUST AUTHORITIES

Law students and beginning lawyers sometimes have a tendency to want to canvass an entire area of law when they do research, instead of focusing their attention on the answers to specific research problems. This seems to stem from a fear that they might miss something if they don't look at all authorities that could even remotely bear on their issue. The problem with this approach is that you can get yourself into a quagmire; the further you go in looking at tangential issues, the harder it is to find your way out of the mess. Law is an interconnected web, and you will always find one more angle to look at if you don't keep your attention focused on solving your specific research problem.

As discussed in Chapter 4, there are better ways to make sure you are not missing important authorities than collecting every case that could possibly be relevant and then trying to sort through them all. (*See also* Chapter 7, section I, for more on overcoming the fear of missing an important case.) While it is important to be persistent and redundant in your research efforts if your initial searches are not productive (*see* section I below), there is no reason to look at every case remotely connected to the general topic if your initial searches are productive and lead you to cases that are on point and factually apposite to your research problem. Instead, you should follow the procedure in Chapter 4 for expanding and updating your research, which will automatically focus your follow-up research on the authorities that are most relevant to your specific research problem. Your goal is not to prepare a mini-treatise on an area of law, but to advance your client's interests with respect to a specific problem or opportunity.

I. IF AT FIRST YOU DON'T SUCCEED, PERSIST!

The flipside of researching too broadly, which was discussed in the previous section, is the tendency some beginning researchers have to give up too quickly when they don't find answers to their research questions right away. Sometimes you will find the answer to your research problem fairly easily; at other times, it can be quite elusive. No matter how methodical you are in following the research strategy set out in Chapters 1–5, there is no precise formula for solving research problems. Every problem is a little different because the facts of any two cases are invariably different, and you can rarely predict with any great degree of confidence exactly how your research is going to turn out. In those situations where you cannot find anything on point, you need to try different approaches and be redundant in your efforts to locate relevant authorities. (*See* Chapter 7, section D, for more on what you should do if you cannot find any controlling cases on point.)

One time a client hired me to handle an appellate matter before the 10th Circuit Court of Appeals. The company wanted to appeal a summary-judgment order that the trial court had entered against it in a contract dispute. I asked an associate to help me research the opening brief, and after several days of evaluating the facts and researching the law, he reported back to me that the client had no chance of winning on appeal and should not bother pursuing it. I thanked him for his hard work and asked him to dig a little deeper. The associate came back a second time and told me that his follow-up research confirmed his original assessment— that any such appeal would be futile. At that point I explained that the client was paying us a lot of money to make the best arguments we could, and that he really needed to try to find *some* kind of authority to support our position before we just threw in the towel. I suggested some additional avenues to explore and sent the associate back to the library. My third meeting with the associate was the charm. It turned out that the law was not nearly as unfavorable to our client as the associate had originally thought, particularly in light of the vague language of the controlling contract. Using the new research he found, I was able to craft a good argument that the contractual language was ambiguous on a key point and should be construed in favor of our client, since the other company had drafted the agreement. The court agreed with this argument and reversed the summary judgment order that the trial court had entered against our client.

Stories like this one underscore the importance of not rushing to the conclusion that there are no authorities on point when you research an issue, particularly when the stakes are high. And they remind me what a curmudgeonly old friend of mine used to tell young lawyers that worked for him: "I didn't hire you to tell me how to lose the case—I can do that myself; just tell me what I need to know in order to win!"

You don't always need to have a controlling authority on point. Sometimes you can use cases from another jurisdiction as persuasive authorities when there are no controlling authorities on point; sometimes you can use secondary as persuasive authorities; and sometimes you can argue by analogy to related areas of law. (*See* Chapter 7, section G for more on using persuasive authorities.) Think creatively: law is as much an art as a science. And keep open the lines of communication with your supervisor when your research doesn't go as planned. Your supervisor is in a better position than you to judge whether a given project merits additional research, and she may well have some good advice on different approaches to try. Remember also that it is persistence that most often separates the first-rate researcher from the average researcher.

J. SHEPARDIZE OR PERISH

There is another bit of advice that *should* go without saying, but I would be remiss if I did not say it again: you absolutely *must* validate the authorities you rely on with a citator before you turn in your final work product. There are no exceptions to this rule.

Failing to validate your authorities is a serious omission that can get you in big trouble. Once, when I was an associate, my firm had an important, emergency hearing in federal court in a case that was well-publicized by the local media. A small team of us put together a lengthy brief in a short time frame, and it was filed with the judge the afternoon before the hearing. The next day, just as the hearing was about to begin, a young lawyer who was in charge of researching a portion of the brief announced frantically that he had discovered an error in his research. It turns out that one of the main cases we were basing our argument on in the brief was no longer valid because it relied upon a statute that had subsequently been repealed. Had the young associate validated the statute before turning in his research, as he should have, he would have seen that the statute had been repealed, but apparently he didn't realize that statutes need to be validated as well as cases. As a result, someone had to take a note to our lead lawyer—while he was in the hearing—informing him that he could not rely on this case that was one of the cornerstones of our argument. Suffice it to say, it was not a happy day for the young associate.

So make sure you validate (using Shepard's or KeyCite) all of your statutes, cases, and regulations before you finalize your research results. If you are not sure whether you did this earlier in your research, or if any significant amount of time has passed since you last did it, then you should validate them again to be on the safe side. The peace of mind you buy will be well worth the small additional outlay of time and money.

Chapter 7

TROUBLE–SHOOTING GUIDE

A. "I'm Not Sure How to Get Started on My Research Project."
B. "I Don't Know Whether I Should Research a Given Project in the Library or on My Computer."
C. "I Don't Know How Much Time I Should Devote to a Given Project."
D. "I'm Not Finding Any Authorities on Point."
E. "My Electronic Word–Searches Are Yielding Too Many Cases to Sort Through Efficiently."
F. "I'm Half–Way Through My Research Project and I'm Really Starting to Feel Confused."
G. "I'm Not Confident in How to Use Persuasive Authorities."
   1. When to Use Persuasive Authorities
   2. Which Persuasive Authorities to Use
   3. Finding Persuasive Cases
H. "I'm Not Sure When or How I Should End My Research."
I. "I'm Afraid That I Might Have Missed an Important Authority."
J. "I Don't Know How to Organize the Results of My Research for My Final Work Product."

Sometimes, even the best legal researchers encounter problems. The 5–step strategy discussed in Chapters 1–5 will help you find solutions to legal research problems efficiently and accurately, but it will not immunize you completely from the types of frustrations every legal researcher deals with from time to time. This section discusses some of the more common obstacles you may expect to encounter, and the ways to get around them. The choice of topics is based in large part on input I have received from law students and beginning lawyers as to the types of problems that they have encountered in their research efforts.

A. "I'M NOT SURE HOW TO GET STARTED ON MY RESEARCH PROJECT."

To begin with, if you haven't read the first chapter of this book, you'll want to do so. As that chapter discusses at length, you need to develop a *research plan* at the beginning of your project. Before you begin looking for authorities that address your research problem, you should think carefully about the precise *question(s)* you need to answer and the *research path* that you think will get you to that answer. You'll also need to think carefully about generating *search terms* and *electronic word-searches* that will enable you to access the various sources of law.

But assuming you have followed **Step 1** carefully and are still unsure where to begin, chances are that you either: (1) are unsure what exactly you are supposed to be looking for, or (2) do not know enough about the particular area of law you are researching to make a reasonable assessment as to the types of authorities that are likely to control the analysis.

The first problem—not being confident in what you are looking for—generally arises because you do not have a meeting of minds with the supervisor who gave you the assignment. Perhaps your supervisor was very busy at the time you met and didn't have time to explain a project in depth. Or perhaps you got nervous because you were working with a particular senior lawyer for the first time, and this nervousness interfered with your listening comprehension. But in any event, you always want to be on the same page with your supervisor on what exactly you are supposed to be researching. If you feel uncertain during your initial meeting as to the nature of the assignment, make sure you ask clarifying questions at that time. It is natural to avoid such questions for fear of appearing ignorant, but the downsides of turning in a poor work product far outweigh this concern. Furthermore, you shouldn't be afraid to go back to your supervisor in the middle of your research project if have lingering doubts about the direction of your research. You don't want to go overboard and make yourself a pest, or ask the same questions repeatedly (remember, take notes!), but seasoned lawyers understand that summer associates and beginning lawyers may need a little guidance as they proceed with a project. Maintaining good communication with your supervisor as you progress through your research can save you a lot of time and needless stress (*see also* Chapter 6, section B.)

The second problem—not knowing enough about an area of law to know where to look for authorities—can be resolved by obtaining some additional background information about your specific problem and about the area of law you have been assigned to research. First, it is helpful to review some of the important documents in the *client file*, such as the pleadings and briefs in a litigation matter, or the agreements and correspondence in a transactional matter. The factual background you obtain will help to put your research issue into context. Second, in order to gain general background information on an unfamiliar area of law, you should consult one or more *secondary sources*. A brief review of an appropriate secondary source can help you frame your research problem and sort out related issues. Often the key to gaining clarity on your research assignment is just to analyze carefully how your precise question presented differs from related legal questions. (*See* Chapter 2, section A, for more on using secondary sources to obtain background information on a topic.)

Finally, you shouldn't hesitate to talk with colleagues if you feel uncertain about a research problem. If you have a real-estate problem and you have a friend in the firm who practices real-estate law, that person should be able to point you in the right direction. Furthermore, a colleague may be able to examine your research problem from a different angle or suggest an approach you hadn't thought about, and often the mere exercise of talking through a problem and explaining it to someone else can help you focus your own thoughts. So don't underestimate the importance of networking—even in your own firm, and even when you are just starting out in the practice of law. Fostering a few mutually supportive relationships can go a long way toward helping both you and your friends advance in your careers.

B. "I DON'T KNOW WHETHER I SHOULD RESEARCH A GIVEN PROJECT IN THE LIBRARY OR ON MY COMPUTER."

The appropriate roles of on-line and library research have been hotly debated since Westlaw and Lexis first came upon the legal scene in the early 1980's. It was apparent to everyone from the start that Westlaw and Lexis could save researchers significant time with certain research tasks, so their value was pretty obvious. Yet there were also a lot of detractors in the early days who believed that while computer research had its place, it should be limited to certain functions, such as pulling up cases and Shepardizing them. Some of that reticence, as you might expect, was based upon the natural reluctance some of us who have been around a while tend to have toward doing things differently from the way we've always done them. Some of it was based on legitimate concerns about the limitations of Westlaw and Lexis in their early forms. And some of it was upon cost considerations and a legitimate concern that young lawyers would rely too heavily on electronic word-searches at the expense of other resources. (Of course, the latter argument is not a legitimate reason to steer beginning lawyers away from computer research *per se*; it is merely a reason to stress to them the importance of following a sound research strategy, such as the one set out in Chapters 1–5 of this book, so that they don't rely exclusively for their research on hastily devised electronic word-searches.)

The situation today, however, is quite different. As lawyers trained on Westlaw and Lexis have assumed their places in the upper echelons of the legal system, the natural resistance to technological change has greatly ebbed. Additionally, Westlaw and Lexis have made significant strides in expanding their coverage and improving their capabilities since the early days, so a lot of the legitimate early criticism is now moot. The advent of the internet has also had a big impact. A lawyer can now do computer research at home, in the office, or even at the beach, whereas the original Westlaw and Lexis terminals were confined to law-library cubicles. In recent years there has also been a proliferation of free material available on the internet that could only be found in law libraries in the early days of computer research. And there are now additional commercial services besides Westlaw and Lexis that generally offer lower prices (though also less-comprehensive services). (For more on the differences between commercial on-line-research services, *see* Chapter 6, section C.)

So really the question these days comes down to this: is it cost-effective to do a particular research project on-line, and if so, is there some other reason why you would want or need to do your research using print sources in a library? Computer research, in other words, has largely become the default option for most lawyers. There are certainly still some resources that are available only in print sources (e.g., certain treatises), and this is likely to remain the case for the foreseeable future. And to be sure, many researchers find it easier to review certain types of sources (e.g., codes and multi-volume treatises) in print rather than on a computer screen. (For more on the virtues of library research, *see* Chapter 6, section D.) But for the most part, on-line research is quicker and more convenient. Therefore, as long as you have access to it, and it is cost-efficient (balancing the cost of the on-line service against the time savings), you should feel free to use your computer for as much of your research as you can. Remember, however, that if you have any doubts about the cost-efficiency of a given project, you should discuss the issue with your supervisor before you start your research. (For more on the cost considerations affecting legal research, *see* Chapter 6, section C.)

On the other hand, if you prefer library research, that is generally fine as well. There are definitely times when you should *not* do your research in print sources because it is inefficient to do so. If, for example, you have to drive across town to look at a resource in a library that you could look up right away on a free on-line site, it is hardly reasonable to pursue the print source.

Likewise, it would rarely make sense to Shepardize cases in the books, since the extra billable time would likely exceed the small on-line charge. But normally, the choice between computer research and library research comes down to a matter of balancing convenience, cost, and personal preference. So if you prefer to read A.L.R.'s articles in print instead of on-line, by all means enjoy your time in the library. In fact, there are sometimes advantages to being a little "old school" in life, and it may just warm the heart of that (super) senior partner down the hall to see you enjoying yourself in the firm's law library instead of gazing at the ubiquitous computer screen. After all, the firm has made a big investment in its library, and it is desirable to let the partners see that their hard-earned money is going to good use.

Regardless of your personal preference for books or computers, however, you should become skilled at using both. Certainly the expectation today is that a beginning lawyer will be proficient at on-line research, and you can advance your career by pursuing advanced Westlaw and Lexis classes, and otherwise honing your electronic research skills. But, it also pays to know your way around a library (*see* Chapter 6, section D). So while as a matter of personal preference you may gravitate toward either on-line research or library research, there will be times when it makes more sense to use the other. Therefore, you need to be proficient at both print and electronic research if you want to be a first-rate researcher.

C. "I DON'T KNOW HOW MUCH TIME I SHOULD DEVOTE TO A GIVEN PROJECT."

This is a common problem for newer lawyers. In law school, you always had a definite deadline for your projects; in practice, you may not. But if you don't have a strict deadline, how do you know if you are putting too much time into a research project or not enough? To a large extent, this turns on the importance of the project. If you are just looking for an authority to support a peripheral point in a brief, you obviously do not want to spend as much time turning over every stone in search of the perfect case as you would if you were researching the decisive issue in the litigation.

Your reasonable expectations based on your background knowledge of the law should also guide you. If you are quite sure that an area of law (say, for example, a tort action for false imprisonment), is governed by state decisional law rather than state statutory law, you would probably be justified in undertaking only a cursory search of the state code just to make sure there were no statutes on point. But if you are quite sure there is a state statute that addresses the issue, then you should keep digging, even if you do not find anything on point right away. For this reason, it is important to educate yourself through secondary sources so you understand the basic legal framework before you start looking for authorities. (For more on using secondary sources to obtain background information on an area of law, *see* Chapter 2, section A.)

It is also important, when you are a newer lawyer especially, to keep your supervisor apprised of your efforts. There is nothing wrong with asking at the beginning of the project how much time the supervisor anticipates that the project should take. The supervisor may in fact say that she just wants you to take a quick look at something, or that she just wants you to spend a few hours researching an area of law. Don't disregard these directions. Lawyers don't like it when they ask an associate to take a quick look at an issue, and then they see at the end of the month when examining the billings that it took the associate 50 billable hours to complete the task. Make sure that you have some idea of the supervisor's expectations regarding time at the beginning of the project, and check back with a progress report if the project seems to be taking longer than expected.

Finally, assuming you keep in mind the considerations discussed above, the short answer to how much time you should spend on a given project is this: as much time as you need to finish the project. That, of course, raises a further question: how do I know when I am finished with my research? That issue is discussed below in section H of this chapter.

D. "I'M NOT FINDING ANY AUTHORITIES ON POINT."

Sometimes the reason beginning lawyers can't find any controlling authorities on point is that there simply aren't any. But often it is because: (1) they are confused about the law and are looking for authorities in the wrong places; (2) their search terms and/or electronic word-searches are inadequate; or (3) they are not extrapolating broadly enough from their research results. So, before you stop researching and conclude that there are no authorities on point, you need to make sure that you've addressed these three possibilities.

You first want to make sure you understand the basic legal framework of your problem and give some thought to where you are likely to find controlling authorities. For this it is helpful to go back to secondary sources to place your legal topic in its larger context. You should be able to tell from your review of secondary sources what types of authorities are likely to control the analysis, and where you are likely to find them. Suppose, for example, that your client owns a shopping center and wants to know whether the shopping center is legally prohibited from leasing space to a gun retailer. Now if you start searching for federal cases to see whether there are any legal restrictions on the ability of shopping centers to lease space to gun retailers, you are likely to come up empty because any restrictions of this type are likely to be found at the local level, not at the federal level. No matter how good your search terms and electronic word-searches are, your searches will be unsuccessful because you are searching in the wrong source. What you should do is locate the applicable municipal code and the local zoning regulations and review their restrictions on commercial leasing. (*See* Chapter 9, section G, for more on re-searching local law.) A good secondary source, such as a treatise on commercial real estate, can re-focus your research and ensure that you are looking in the right places for relevant primary authorities. (For more on using secondary sources to re-focus your research, *see* Chapter 2, section E.)

A second reason why lawyers sometimes have trouble finding any controlling authorities on point is that their search terms and/or their electronic word-searches are too narrow. The solution in that event, of course, is to try formulating some additional searches. If you are researching in print, you may need to use broader search terms or think of broader concepts when you access tables of contents or indexes; if you are researching on-line using electronic word-searches, you can broaden your searches by using broader search terms, fewer search terms, and less-restrictive terms and connectors. (For more on how to improve your search terms and your electronic word-searches, *see* Chapter 1, section B.) You can also try running some electronic word-searches if you have been searching solely in print sources, and vice versa. Terms-and-connectors searches allow you to hone in on issues with greater precision than is possible using a digest. But on the other hand, electronic word-searches can miss relevant authorities if you do not craft them carefully, so a digest can serve as a check on the reliability of your electronic word-searches. Thus, if you are having trouble finding cases with one tool, you should try the other.

Third, before you conclude that there are no controlling authorities, give some thought to whether the authorities you did find are more on point than you may have assumed. Beginning researchers sometimes make the mistake of thinking that there are no authorities on point because the authorities they have found are not precisely on par factually with their research scenarios. But often this just means that they need to *extrapolate* a bit from the existing authorities to arrive at a reasonable conclusion. You won't often find cases with precisely your fact pattern, but that doesn't necessarily mean that they aren't on point. You may need to think a little more creatively to answer your question(s) presented, taking rules out of their specific factual contexts and applying them in a new context.

To paraphrase a hypothetical the well-known legal philosopher H.L.A. Hart once posed, suppose a certain municipality passes a very basic ordinance: "No vehicles are allowed in Washington Park." Your client wants to operate his vintage moped in the park. You've found three previous decisions on point: one holds that *cars* are "vehicles" within the meaning of the ordinance, one holds that *motorcycles* are "vehicles" within the meaning of the ordinance, and one holds that *bicycles* are **not** "vehicles" within the meaning of the ordinance. So based on the available law, is a moped a "vehicle" within the meaning of the ordinance? Your authorities will not give you a definitive answer to this question because there is no authority precisely on point. So you will need to creatively analyze the authorities you found to determine what you think the likely outcome would be if your client's case were to proceed to litigation. Is a moped operating with its engine on more like a car/motorcycle, or more like a bicycle? What if the operator is merely peddling the moped with the engine off? Does the legal status of a moped change depending on whether the engine is running or not?

So as long as you have been careful in your research and have followed the steps set out in this book, you should not feel befuddled because you cannot find a case that addresses your precise factual situation. Associates get paid the big bucks not just to find the law, but to analyze it and apply it as well. Sometimes you will need to think creatively about the existing authorities you've found and use your best judgment to determine how you think a court would (or should) apply them in your situation. Beginning researchers sometimes find the indefiniteness of the law disconcerting, but in time you will become comfortable with the occasional absence of clear answers to your research problems. This doesn't mean you haven't done a good job on your research; it just means that you can't easily separate legal research from creative legal analysis.

Finally, if you have addressed all three of these potential pitfalls and you still can't find any controlling authorities on point, you will probably want to look for *persuasive authorities* to fill in the void. In fact, you may want to look for persuasive authorities even if you *do* find cases from the controlling jurisdiction that are roughly on point, if, as discussed above, you find it necessary to extrapolate from those cases to reach your conclusion. In that event, finding a case from another state that is more on par factually with your research scenario than the cases from the controlling jurisdiction will help to buttress your conclusion.

(*See* section G of this chapter for more on how to find and use persuasive authorities.)

It is always a good idea to discuss with your supervisor how much additional effort she wants you to devote to a given project before you get too deep into a search for persuasive authorities. But as a rule you should err on the side of persistence when it comes to legal research (*see* Chapter 6, section I.) Spending a little more time on your research than you think you should have is preferable to coming up empty-handed when there are relevant authorities to be had.

E.   "MY ELECTRONIC WORD–SEARCHES ARE YIELDING TOO MANY CASES TO SORT THROUGH EFFICIENTLY."

Sometimes, the problem with using on-line electronic word-searches is not that you cannot find *any* authorities, but that your searches yield *too many* authorities. This makes your research inefficient because you waste time sifting through a lot of irrelevant search results. There are several steps you can take to address this problem.

First, consider whether you can limit your search to a more restrictive database. You obviously don't want to start out searching in an *all-states* database if you are just trying to find Minnesota case law. And you may not even want to use a Minnesota *state and federal* database if you are primarily looking for controlling cases on Minnesota law. Instead, try confining your search to the Minnesota *state cases* database to see if there are any cases on point; if there aren't any, you can always expand your search to Minnesota federal cases for persuasive authority, and if that comes up empty, to cases from other states.

Next, assuming you are searching in the proper database, you should revisit your question presented and make sure that it is not too broad. Are you framing the question narrowly, so that it addresses precisely what you are looking for, or is it a vague, general question? If your question presented is overly broad, your search terms are likely to be overly broad as well. Perhaps you need to be more specific about the factual context of your research problem. You can also use more precise terminology in framing the question presented: try "cat," for example, instead of "animal," and "draft" instead of "negotiable instrument." You may also want to revisit secondary sources to borrow some of the specific terms of art they employ in discussing the subject matter. (For more on using secondary sources to refine your search terms, *see* Chapter 2, section D.) Once your question presented is narrowly framed, then the search terms you derive from the question presented should become more precise as well. (For more on narrowing the scope of your search terms, *see* Chapter 1, section B(1).)

If you are still having problems with the broadness of your electronic word-searches even after you have revisited your database, your question(s) presented, and your search terms, then the problem is likely due to the manner in which you have combined your search terms into electronic word-searches. So you will need to work on formulating more narrowly crafted word-searches. If you are using *natural-language* searches, you should consider using *terms-and-connectors* searches instead, as these give you the ability to formulate very precise searches. (For more on narrowing the scope of your electronic word-searches, *see* Chapter 1, section B(2).)

An alternative way to deal with the problem of too many search results is to use a digest in lieu of electronic word-searches. Digests winnow your search for you. You can start with a broad topic in the index and then look for successively narrower topics until you find a manageable number of annotations. If you are researching on Westlaw or Lexis, you can use the on-line digest function (click *KeySearch* on Westlaw, *Search by Topic or Headnote* on Lexis) to search by topic, drilling down to successively narrower topics until you get to a manageable level of specificity. If the most specific topic is still too broad, you can enter key words to hone the results even further, though usually the most specific sub-topics (at least within a particular jurisdiction) have a manageable number of corresponding annotations. (For more on using digests, *see* Chapter 8, section G(1).)

F. "I'M HALF–WAY THROUGH MY RESEARCH PROJECT AND I'M REALLY STARTING TO FEEL CONFUSED."

For the legal researcher, there is little more frustrating than investing a significant amount of time in a research project, only to feel more uncertain about the solution to the problem than you were at the beginning of the project. But don't worry: it happens to all of us from time to time. You just need to relax, take a few deep breaths, and re-assess the situation.

Generally this problem arises when you haven't really figured out the nuances of your research problem yet, leading you to conflate issues that are closely related, but subtly different. Often this is because you don't understand the *context* of your research well enough. That is, you don't know enough about the general subject matter, and you get confused by the nuances. To remedy this, you first need to gain a better understanding of the broader topic and think about how your topic relates to other topics that are similar, yet different. One good way to gain a better understanding of the context of your research is to go back to *secondary sources* for an overview of the general topic (*see* Chapter 2, section E). As you are doing so, think about how your specific issue fits into a larger legal category, and how it is distinguishable from the other topics in that category. Consider also sketching an outline or a chart that shows how your specific issue fits within the structure of the larger topic. Getting a clearer understanding of the logical relationships between your specific topic and other related topics should help to alleviate your confusion.

Suppose, for example, that you are researching the litigation doctrine of *collateral estoppel,* which is also known as *issue preclusion.* You need to know whether your client, who is the defendant in a lawsuit, is precluded from challenging an adverse factual determination that a judge made in an earlier case involving your client. If you are not conversant with the law governing the preclusive effects of earlier litigation, you may become confused by cases applying similar but subtly different doctrines such as *equitable estoppel* and *claim preclusion*, and you may become further confused by cases discussing *res judicata,* which is sometimes used as a general term encompassing both claim preclusion and issue preclusion, but other times is used as a synonym for claim preclusion alone. By reviewing a good secondary source on civil procedure, such as *Moore's Federal Practice* treatise, and analyzing how these similar concepts relate to one another and how they differ, you can reduce your chances of going off on research tangents that ultimately have no bearing on your problem.

Often the reason researchers confuse related issues that arise in the course of their research projects is that they fail to think through adequately the nuances of their problems at the beginning of their research. It is important to analyze your research problem and plan your research *before* you start looking for primary authorities. (For more on formulating a research plan, *see* Chapter 1, section A). If you don't, you risk confusion in the middle of your project because your broad pursuit of related topics will often get you further and further from the answer you need as you follow up each tangential question that arises.

So if you start feeling confused in the middle of a project, you should, in addition to revisiting secondary sources, revisit your *question presented* and your *initial outline* to make sure that they are as precise as possible and don't conflate related concepts. Try to figure out how your question presented differs from related questions that look at first blush on point, but end up leading you away from your actual topic, and refine the language so that you eliminate any ambiguity. Consider also how the facts that are peculiar to your research problem distinguish your research scenario from some of the tangential cases you will read. Once you get clear on your precise question presented, then your search terms, which flow from the question presented, should likewise become more focused. And this improved focus should help you hone in more accurately on relevant primary authorities.

Finally, there are some common-sense things you can do when you feel confused in the middle of a research project. Often you just need to take a break and do something else to let your unconscious mental processes work on the problem. When you come back to it later, and you are more relaxed, you'll probably find that you see the problem more clearly. It also helps to talk through the problem with a colleague, or perhaps with a research librarian. Not only might that person have some ideas you haven't thought of, but sometimes just explaining the problem to someone else—even without significant input from the person you are talking with—can help you work through the obstacles that have been holding you back. And lastly, relax and remind yourself that what you are experiencing is common. Legal analysis is complicated, and it often yields no clear results; learning to live with uncertainty is just part of the game.

G. "I'M NOT CONFIDENT IN HOW TO USE PERSUASIVE AUTHORITIES."

Beginning lawyers are often uncertain about the role of *persuasive authorities* in their research. (Persuasive authorities, as you recall, are authorities, such as cases from states other than the controlling state, that are not legally binding on a court, but merely provide guidance as to the appropriate way to decide a case.) It is sometimes difficult to know *when* you should rely on persuasive authorities, *which* persuasive authorities you should rely on, or *how* you should go about finding them. This section addresses each of those concerns.

1. When to Use Persuasive Authorities

The basic rule on using persuasive authorities is that you should consider using them when the controlling law in a jurisdiction is unclear. Usually this is because courts in the controlling jurisdiction have simply not had the opportunity to consider the specific legal issue. However, there are other reasons why the law may not be clear. For example, there may be a precedent in the controlling jurisdiction that is roughly on point, but it is not close on the facts to the case at issue. If there is a case in another jurisdiction that reaches a different result and is closer on the facts, you can reasonably argue that a court in the controlling jurisdiction would likely have reached a similar result as the out-of-state case if it had been confronted with similar facts. In that specific factual context, you can argue, the law of the controlling state is unclear, and the reviewing court should look to the out-of-state precedent for guidance. Another reason the law in a particular jurisdiction may be unclear is that there are conflicting decisions in the controlling jurisdiction, and it isn't clear how the cases can be harmonized. For example, there may be decisions from two different appeals-court panels that reach different results, and you cannot easily synthesize a rule from them that would apply in your case. In that scenario, you can look to out-of-state cases or a secondary source for guidance in choosing between the conflicting rules. (For more on dealing with conflicting cases, *see* Chapter 5, section A(2).)

Finally, there are (relatively rare) occasions when you may use persuasive authorities to argue against the law in the controlling jurisdiction, even though it is clear. For example, it may sometimes be worth arguing (particularly if you don't have anything else to rely on) in an appeal before a court of last resort (e.g., a state supreme court) that the established precedent in the jurisdiction (e.g., a decision from the intermediary court of appeals) should be overruled because it is contrary to the majority rule in all or most other jurisdictions, and it is a poorly reasoned decision. To support that type of argument, you will want to cite to well-reasoned cases from other jurisdictions (and perhaps also to certain secondary sources) that are contrary to the controlling precedent.

Depending on the situation, therefore, persuasive authorities can fill a void in the controlling law, add greater specificity to the controlling law, or even serve as a basis for challenging the controlling law. Accordingly, if your research fails to turn up any controlling authorities directly on point, you would *generally* want to look for persuasive authorities to fill the void, particularly if your case is one of first impression in the controlling jurisdiction. (Before you spend a lot of time looking for persuasive authorities, however, you should check with your supervising attorney to make sure that you are both on the same page.)

2.   Which Persuasive Authorities to Use

Once you have decided to look for persuasive authorities to buttress your research, you will need to decide *which* persuasive authorities to rely on. If your research involves statutory interpretation, you may at times want to rely on a model code for persuasive authority, or you may want to rely on the language of a non-controlling statute in the controlling jurisdiction that sheds light on how the controlling statute should be interpreted. If, for example, your research involves the meaning of the term "motor vehicles" in a statute prohibiting the operation of motor vehicles in a park, you may want to look at how the term "motor vehicles" is defined elsewhere in that state's code, if the statutory provision you are interpreting doesn't define it, and there are no cases that interpret the term for you. Perhaps there is a separate statute that prohibits the driving of motor vehicles while intoxicated, and that statute has a definition section that includes the term "motor vehicles." In that scenario, you can look to the definition in the non-controlling statute for guidance in construing the controlling statute. (Note that the same applies for *regulations*: if a certain term is defined in a non-controlling regulation in an administrative code, a court can look to that definition for guidance in construing the same term in a different regulation in the code.)

If it is persuasive *cases* you are looking for and you are researching a matter of *federal law*, you will want to look to decisions from federal district courts and from federal appeals courts outside the controlling circuit. If you are researching a matter of *state law*, you should start by looking for federal cases from the applicable district and circuit that interpret the controlling state's law. While not themselves controlling, federal cases interpreting state law are considered highly persuasive in the absence of controlling decisions from the state's own courts. And if you cannot find any decisions from the federal courts interpreting the state's law, then you will want to look at cases from other states to see if they have addressed the issue.

Keep in mind that not all persuasive cases are of equal weight. A supreme-court decision from another state, for example, is going to carry more weight (other things being equal) than an intermediary court-of-appeals decision from that same state. Likewise, a case that is close on the facts to your case will carry more weight than a comparable case that is factually inapposite. The age of the case will also factor in: generally, the newer the case, the more authoritative it is. And a case supported by sound, detailed reasoning is going to be more authoritative than a short, conclusory opinion. Some judges even take into account the jurisdiction from which the persuasive case arises. For example, a judge in the controlling state may find cases from neighboring states more persuasive than cases from other parts of the country. The justice I clerked for on the Michigan Supreme Court, conversely, favored persuasive decisions from the New York and Massachusetts high courts because of their long-standing, well-developed jurisprudence, and because they had produced some very highly esteemed jurists over the years, such as Benjamin Cardozo and Oliver Wendell Holmes.

The procedural posture of your case will also affect what decisions are most persuasive. For example, if you are before a federal *district court* in the 8th Circuit, that court may regard decisions from other district courts within the 8th Circuit as more persuasive than the decisions of U.S. courts of appeals from outside the 8th Circuit. Conversely, if your case is on appeal to the 8th Circuit, that court will likely regard the relevant decisions of other U.S. courts of appeals to be more persuasive than the decisions of district courts within the 8th Circuit.

So a number of factors can have an influence on the weight courts give a particular persuasive case. You will need to consider them carefully when choosing which cases to use for your analysis. (For more on choosing which authorities to rely on in your analysis, *see* Chapter 5, section A(2)(a).)

3. Finding Persuasive Cases

Finding persuasive cases basically involves the same process as finding cases from the controlling jurisdiction (*see* Chapter 3, section B(3)). First, you can revisit secondary sources to see if you can find a discussion of your issue; if so, they will likely refer you to at least some cases from various jurisdictions that have addressed the issue. An A.L.R. annotation is probably the most useful secondary source for this purpose, if you can locate one on point, since A.L.R. annotations provide a plethora of case references to various jurisdictions. If you cannot locate an A.L.R. annotation on point, try a loose-leaf service if you are researching a specialized area of law, or try one of the Restatements or a multi-volume treatise if you are researching a more general topic. All of these secondary sources contain numerous cites to cases from a variety of jurisdictions.

You can also use West's Digest System to look for cases in other jurisdictions by topic. If you have already found a case in the controlling jurisdiction that is roughly on point (but perhaps not quite factually on par), you can use the *key number* for the topic to find cases from other jurisdictions that are more on point. Look at *West's Federal Practice Digest* if you are searching for persuasive federal cases; look in one or more of West's *regional digests* or in *West's General Digest* (using the *decennial digests* to find earlier cases) if you are searching for persuasive cases from state courts. If you do not already have a case that is roughly on point, you can look up the relevant topic in the *Descriptive Word Index* that accompanies the digest.

If you are researching on *Westlaw* and you have a case roughly on point, you can just click on the relevant key number in the headnotes and then select *All* (or a particular jurisdiction) to find cases from other jurisdictions on the same topic. And if you do not already have a case roughly on point, you can click on the *Key Numbers* tab at the top of the page to search for key numbers by topic. If you are researching on *Lexis* and already have a case roughly on point, you can use the *More Like This* function to find cases from other jurisdictions on the same topic. If you do not already have a case roughly on point, you can use the *Search by Topic or Headnote* function to search for cases from other jurisdictions by topic. Both Westlaw and Lexis allow you to customize your search by adding your own search terms. (For more on finding cases using digests, *see* Chapter 8, section G(1).)

The third—and probably the easiest—way to find persuasive cases on a certain topic is simply to run the same electronic word-searches you ran in your search for controlling authorities on that topic, only this time using a combined database. Lexis and West-law both have various combined databases that allow you to search for all federal cases, all state cases, or combined federal and state cases. Just select the appropriate database and run your same search. Assuming your search for cases in the controlling jurisdiction came up dry because of an absence of case law rather than a poorly structured word-search (*see* section D of this chapter if you are not sure), you should be able to quickly locate any cases on point from other jurisdictions. On the other hand, if you end up having to modify your original electronic word-search to find cases on point from other jurisdictions, make sure you try the successful, modified word-search in the controlling jurisdiction as well, just to make sure your failure to find controlling cases there was not the result of a defective electronic word-search.

Once you find persuasive cases that address your topic, you can use them both to predict what a court in the controlling jurisdiction would likely decide if confronted with your specific issue, and to influence the court's decision if the matter proceeds to litigation. After all, even though persuasive cases are not binding on the courts, respect for precedent runs deep in the judicial temperament.

Finally, *secondary sources* can also serve as persuasive authorities in certain circumstances. Most commonly, you would use a secondary source as a persuasive authority either to establish the majority rule on a particular point of law, or to persuade a court that a certain position is better reasoned or more in keeping with a current trend in the law than an alternative position. On rare occasion, you might even need to rely on a secondary authority alone because there are not even any persuasive cases available, as in a new or rapidly changing area of law.

Like cases from other jurisdictions, secondary sources vary as to their authoritativeness when used as persuasive authorities. Courts give some of them, such as the Restatements and certain well-respected treatises, a significant amount of weight, while others, such as ALR's and legal encyclopedias, are not considered very authoritative. (*See* Chapter 2, section B, and Chapter 8 for more on using individual secondary sources as persuasive authorities.)

H.   "I'M NOT SURE WHEN OR HOW I SHOULD END MY RESEARCH."

Beginning researchers often feel uneasy about terminating their research because there are always additional stones that can be over-turned when you are searching for legal authorities. Sometimes the end game will be determined for you—where, for example, your supervisor tells you to spend an hour looking at a particular topic and report back. But more typically, you will have to develop a feel for when you have researched thoroughly enough that you feel confident in your analysis without having to look further. Generally this takes a fair amount of research practice. But there are some steps you can take to hasten the process.

First, you need to get in the habit of doing thorough, efficient research. If you have followed the five steps set out in Chapters 1–5 of this book, you should feel confident that you have done everything you needed to do to find a solution to your research problem. If you haven't already done so, read Chapter 5, which deals with the steps you need to take to finalize your research.

Usually what beginning lawyers mean when they say they don't know how to end their research is that they don't know if they should keep executing additional searches, looking for more or better authorities. The answer to that question depends in large part on how successful your existing searches have been. If, after a thorough search following **Steps 1–3**, you've successfully found primary authorities that directly answer your question(s) presented, then you can move on to **Step 4** (*see* Chapter 4) to expand and update your case research. You don't need to look for every case that could possibly relate to the topic (*see also* Chapter 6, section H).

Let's say, for example, that after a thorough search for primary authorities, you find one controlling case that directly answers your question presented. At that point I would first review the precedents that are cited *within* the controlling case to see if any of them are on point. If so, then I would include them in my research results. Next I would perform a *key-number search* within the controlling jurisdiction to make sure there were no other important cases on point that I (and the controlling case) had missed. Then I would use a *citator* to see if there were any more recent cases that cited the controlling case. (And if some of my newly discovered cases are on point, I would need to Shepard-ize them as well, together with any new cases they cite that are on point.) At that juncture I would generally feel pretty confident in moving on to **Step 5** to finalize my research.

If your searches have *not* been very successful in answering your question presented, it gets a little trickier knowing when to quit. As discussed in Chapter 6, section I, you want to be persistent and try different approaches if you are not finding any controlling authorities directly on point. But if you've done this, and each different approach keeps leading you back to the same principles and the same marginally relevant cases, you can take that as a pretty reliable indicator that you haven't overlooked any important cases. And if you then expand and update your case research as described in the previous paragraph, and the additional cases you find are even less relevant to your research problem than the cases you've already found, then that is further confirmation that you haven't missed any significant cases. At that point, you can end your search for controlling cases and consider (in consultation with your supervisor) whether you want to continue your research by looking for *persuasive authorities*. (For more on the decision whether to search for persuasive authorities, *see* Chapter 5, section A(3), along with section G(1) of this chapter.)

I. "I'M AFRAID THAT I MIGHT HAVE MISSED AN IMPORTANT AUTHORITY."

Unfortunately, there are no guarantees in legal research. However, if you have followed the suggestions set out in Chapters 1–5 of this book, you shouldn't have a problem. The important things to keep in mind are that you need to be *thorough* in your research, and that you should stress *redundancy* if you have any concerns about the completeness of your research (*see* Chapter 6, section I). You also need to make sure that you properly *expand and update* your research, as discussed in Chapter 4.

Being *thorough* in your research means taking the time to work through each of the steps discussed in Chapters 1–5. Admittedly, you may find an answer to a research problem more quickly if, for example, you don't take the time to sketch a research plan, or if you skip the important step of reviewing one or more secondary sources. And to be sure, there may be occasions when you are forced by time constraints to abbreviate your normal research process. But it is at these times that you run the highest risk of missing something important, so unless you are facing an urgent time constraint, it is generally not worth running that risk. Therefore, if you are concerned about missing a key authority, first make sure that you haven't short-circuited your research strategy for the sake of expediency.

Second, it helps to be *redundant* in your research. Look at more than one secondary source, for example, if you don't feel comfortable with the area of law you are researching. Check the A.L.R.'s, look for a law-review article, try to find a relevant loose-leaf service. You can also be redundant in your search for primary authorities. Instead of relying solely on an annotated code to find cases interpreting a statute, try using a citator as well (which will also ensure that you find the most recent cases). Instead of relying solely on electronic word-searches to find relevant cases, try looking at a digest too. If you take more than one approach to finding legal authorities, and they lead you to the same results, you can be pretty confident that you have not missed anything important.

Finally, you need to make sure that you properly expand and update your research, as discussed in Chapter 4. This is a crucial step that many law students skip. For example, you need to make sure that you've used a citator not only to check whether your cases are still good law, but also to check whether there are more recent cases on point. You need to do this for all of your cases that are on point, and you need to keep doing it with each new case you find that is on point until there are no more recent citing cases to look at. (*See* Chapter 4, section C, for more on using a citator to expand and update your research.)

In sum, you can never be absolutely certain that your research is impeccable; unfortunately, a degree of uncertainty is just part of the game. But if you are thorough in your research strategy (including your review of secondary sources), redundant in your approach when faced with uncertainty, and careful to expand and update your research, you can have a high degree of confidence that you have not missed any key authorities.

J. "I DON'T KNOW HOW TO ORGANIZE THE RESULTS OF MY RESEARCH FOR MY FINAL WORK PRODUCT."

It is important to organize your research results not only at the end of your project, but throughout the course of your research. Basically this involves undertaking two tasks early in your research process. First, you need to prepare an *initial outline* of the major issues after you have reviewed secondary sources in **Step 2**, and you need to revise this outline as you progress with your research. (For more on preparing and revising your initial outline, *see* Chapter 3, section A.) Second, you need to keep good *records* of your research as you progress, and you need to "link" each authority you find that you intend to rely on in your analysis to one or more of the points in your outline. (For more on the importance of keeping good records as you research, *see* Chapter 6, section E). If you do these things, it should be fairly easy to finalize your outline after you have completed your research, and from there it should be relatively easy to prepare your final work product. (For more on finalizing your research, *see* Chapter 5, section B.)

Part III

THE PRINCIPAL SOURCES OF LAW—AN OVERVIEW

The focus of this book is on legal research *strategy,* rather than on the process of researching individual sources of law. I am assuming that you have already learned how to work with the various sources of law. For purposes of reference, however, this part of the book provides a short summary of the principal legal sources and their uses. For further reference, there are several helpful texts you can consult to learn more about finding and working with the individual sources of law, such as Kent C. Olson's newly revised *Principles of Legal Research.* Check with your law librarian for additional recommendations.

Sources of law are conventionally catalogued into two groups: *secondary sources* and *primary sources.* In a nutshell, secondary sources contain commentary on the law, whereas primary sources contain the law itself. Both are important to legal research. Chapter 8 summarizes secondary sources, and Chapter 9 summarizes primary sources. Most of these sources are available on Lexis, Westlaw, and the other commercial on-line services, as well as in print. Many of them are also available on free websites, such as the websites for Cornell Law School's Legal Information Institute (www.law.cornell.edu), American Law Sources On–Line (www.lawsource.com), Google Scholar (www.scholar.google.com), and FindLaw (www.lp.findlaw.com). These free on-line resources tend to be somewhat limited in their coverage, however, particularly with regard to secondary sources, and they generally lack the sophisticated search capabilities of Lexis and Westlaw. So you will probably not be able to rely on them exclusively for all of your research needs. Remember to check with your reference librarian if you cannot locate a particular source.

Chapter 8

SECONDARY SOURCES OF LAW

Secondary sources are not themselves legal authorities, but rather reference works designed to explain the law and to help you locate primary authorities. Related to these are *finding tools*, such as digests and case citators, which do not provide any background or commentary on the law but simply direct the user to primary sources of law. For the sake of convenience, digests and citators are summarized in this chapter along with secondary sources. The principal secondary sources and finding tools you are likely to use in the practice of law are discussed below.

A. LEGAL ENCYCLOPEDIAS

Legal encyclopedias are like any other encyclopedia. They summarize the law by topic, and the topics are arranged alphabetically. There are two main types of legal encyclopedias: one focuses on general legal principles common to most jurisdictions, while the other type is jurisdiction-specific. There are two principal general-law encyclopedias: American Jurisprudence 2d ("Am. Jur.") and Corpus Juris Secundum ("C.J.S."). Many states have their own jurisdiction-specific encyclopedias; these are often more helpful than the general-law encyclopedias for providing background on state-specific research problems.

Encyclopedias are easy to use. If you have a broad topic, you may find it listed alphabetically on the spine of one of the individual volumes. If you have a more specific issue, you should use the topical index. Legal encyclopedias have extensive topical indexes arranged alphabetically, which you can access with your search terms (*see* Chapter 1, section B(1)). If you are researching on Westlaw or Lexis, you can also search for topics within the encyclopedia by using electronic word-searches (*see* Chapter 1, section B(2)). Remember that you will need to check the pocket parts of individual volumes for updates if you are researching an encyclopedia in print form, just as you do for most print sources.

Encyclopedias are useful for obtaining very basic background information on a topic, particularly in cases where you know little about the area of law and just need a broad overview. Generally, however, they do not provide detailed enough information to be more than a starting point for your secondary-source research.

Encyclopedias can sometimes be useful for finding primary authorities; state-specific encyclopedias are helpful in that regard if you are researching an issue of state law.

Encyclopedias are not regarded as scholarly works, so they are not generally cited as persuasive authorities. On rare occasions, the general-law encyclopedias (i.e., Am. Jur. and C.J.S.) can be helpful as persuasive authorities where you simply want to describe what the majority rule is among the states on a general, well-established point of law, and you cannot locate a more authoritative source (e.g., a multi-volume treatise or a Restatement) on point. But most of the time you will want to cite to a more authoritative source.

B. TREATISES AND PRACTICE MANUALS

Treatises and practice manuals are reference works that summarize and provide information on individual areas of law. While there are no hard and fast distinctions between the two, most librarians use the term "treatises" to refer to more scholarly works that contain critical commentary and analysis, as well as background information, historical information, and references to primary materials. They have traditionally been written by law professors and are frequently contained in multi-volume collections. "Practice manuals" are similar to treatises, but as the name suggests, they have a more practical orientation. They focus on providing assistance to the practitioner in understanding and using the law, rather than generating scholarly commentary. Practice manuals can be either single-volume or multi-volume works; the latter are sometimes published on 3–ring binders. They are usually written by practitioners—sometimes by groups of practitioners that have different sub-specialties.

Practice manuals are generally more specialized than treatises. Some of them (*state practice manuals*) are state-specific in their focus, while others (*specialized practice manuals*) are multi-jurisdictional but have a narrow subject-matter focus, such as federal securities regulation or commercial-zoning law. Practitioners in relatively arcane areas of the law have increasingly come to rely on specialized practice manuals, along with loose-leaf services (which are discussed in section F of this chapter) because they collect in one place various types of primary and secondary authorities relevant to the specialty, in addition to providing helpful background information about the primary authorities. State practice manuals make a useful tool if you are researching issues of state law because they provide background information on the specifics of state law, as well as citations to key primary authorities in the relevant state. Both types of practice manuals provide practical guidance and tips for practitioners, such as how to prepare various types of documents.

Treatises and practice manuals explain and analyze the law in more detail than encyclopedias. Therefore, it is usually better to use a treatise or practice manual rather than an encyclopedia to learn about an area of the law, unless you just need a cursory overview of a general legal topic before you undertake more detailed research. Treatises and practice manuals are also helpful for finding primary authorities; this is particularly true of practice manuals because they are narrower in their focus. And finally, when used appropriately, treatises make good persuasive authorities in situations where you cannot find primary authorities on point (*see* Chapter 2, section C). This is particularly true when the treatises are complex, multi-volume works, when the authors are well-known and respected scholars, and when the treatises are kept up to date. Practice manuals are cited as persuasive authorities less frequently than treatises because they generally lack critical commentary and analysis.

Treatises and practice manuals are easy to access. As with legal encyclopedias, you can use your search terms to access the topical index. Just remember that you may need to narrow or broaden those terms (*see* Chapter 1, section B(1)) if you do not find what you are looking for in the index. If you are researching on-line, you can also use full-text electronic word-searches to customize your search. Lexis and Westlaw each carry a good selection of major treatises in their collections of secondary materials, so you may be able to find what you are looking for there. Be aware, however, that the two services carry somewhat different collections, so if you cannot find a specific treatise on one, you may want to check the other service as well. If you are researching in print sources, or you cannot locate a treatise you want on either Westlaw or Lexis, check the subject index of your law library to see what is available in print. When choosing a treatise, make sure that it is one that is updated regularly, or it may no longer be reliable.

C. LEGAL PERIODICALS

Articles in legal periodicals serve a similar function as treatises, but they are even more narrowly focused in terms of subject matter. They offer detailed treatment of individual topics, but the publishers do not attempt to canvas the whole of the law, as legal encyclopedias do, or even entire areas of the law, as treatises do. So depending on your topic, you may or may not find an article on point.

There are two main types of articles that are useful for legal research: law-review articles and bar-journal articles. Law-review articles, generally written by academics, tend to be significantly more detailed, but they are sometimes too theoretical to meet the needs of practitioners. Bar-journal articles, on the other hand, which are generally written by practitioners, are more practical. For example, they may provide advice on how to draft a certain type of document. But they are often too cursory to be very useful for in-depth legal research. Bar-journal articles are more likely to be jurisdiction-specific, whereas law-review articles tend to focus on general legal principles. Thus, it is usually best to look for a state bar-journal article if you are researching a routine matter of state law, and to look for a law-review article if you have a novel issue or one that cuts across multiple jurisdictions.

Both bar-journal articles and law-review articles can provide useful background information on the topics they cover, as well as references to relevant primary authorities. In addition, a law-review article from a respected author that is right on point can make an excellent persuasive authority, particularly in a new or unsettled area of law.

Legal-periodical articles are not difficult to find. Most articles that you would find useful for practical research are available through commercial on-line services such as Westlaw and Lexis.

You can find them either through topical indexes or through electronic word-searches. If you are researching in a library, you can use either *LegalTrac* or the *Index to Legal Periodicals and Books* to locate articles in print form. *HeinOnline* is another helpful resource that carries an extensive collection of law-review articles, along with a variety of other legal materials. It is a subscription service, but most law libraries have access to it. HeinOnline is useful because its coverage of legal periodicals extends further back in time, making it a valuable resource for historical research.

You can use the search terms that you generated in **Step 1** of your research to find articles relevant to your topic (*see* Chapter 1, section B(1)). Keep in mind that articles are not updated, so you will need to consider whether a particular article is still accurate, particularly if you plan to use it as a persuasive authority.

D. A.L.R.'S

American Law Reports is the name of a publication that has been around for nearly a century. It publishes "annotations," which are basically articles that focus on the cases across the country that deal with various legal topics. Typically, an A.L.R annotation will discuss one case in detail by way of example, and then briefly summarize all the other cases nationally that discuss the same issue. The cases are broken down by jurisdiction, and the annotation will generally try to distill a majority rule from the cases. A.L.R.'s are organized by series (e.g., A.L.R.1st, A.L.R.2d, etc.), with the first series containing the earliest annotations, and the highest-number series containing the most recent annotations. A.L.R.'s are continually updated with supplemental volumes, so even the earliest annotations will refer you to recent cases, unless, as occasionally happens, they have been superseded by later annotations. Separate series of annotations (A.L.R. Fed and A.L.R. Fed2d) are devoted to discussions of federal cases.

Print versions of the A.L.R.'s can be accessed through indexes; to access the on-line versions, you can run electronic word-searches, using the search terms you generated in **Step 1** (*see* Chapter 1, section B(1)). The A.L.R.'s also contain tables of authorities that allow you to search for annotations that discuss a particular case, statute, or regulation. Remember that if you are researching in print, you will need to check the supplements and pocket parts to find the most recent cases.

A.L.R. annotations often provide a significant amount of helpful information on the topics they discuss, though there is no guarantee that you will find an annotation on any particular topic. Nevertheless, if you do find an annotation on point, it can be quite valuable, both for providing an overview of the topic and the manner in which courts have addressed it, and for the detailed references it provides to primary authorities. A.L.R. annotations also contain a wealth of information on the other secondary sources available on a given topic. So if you have a complicated research topic, it is generally worth taking a look at the A.L.R indexes to see if there are any annotations on point.

You may also find a reference to a useful A.L.R. annotation in another secondary source, or through an on-line search for cases. Westlaw, for example, automatically generates cites to relevant secondary sources, including A.L.R. annotations, when it displays search results for cases, through its *ResultsPlus* feature. Lexis does the same through its *Related Content* feature.

A.L.R. annotations are not particularly authoritative when used as persuasive authorities, since they merely catalog cases and do not analyze legal trends or provide commentary. However, they are occasionally cited in briefs to establish what the majority rule is among the various states that have addressed a particular issue, if there is no more authoritative source on point, such as a multi-volume treatise.

E. RESTATEMENTS OF THE LAW

The Restatements of Law are compilations of rules, illustrations and commentary that are prepared by the American Law Institute to organize and clarify the principles of the common law. The Restatements are broken down by subject matter (e.g., torts, trusts and estates, contracts), and there are three series: the original Restatements, the Restatements of the Law (Second), and the Restatements of the Law (Third). The third series is a continuing work in progress. The second and third series of Restatements include annotations (i.e., short summaries) of all the cases that have cited the various sections of the Restatements. These can be found in multi-volume appendices to the main Restatement volumes. The individual Restatements are organized by section number. Each Restatement has a topical index that allows you to find relevant sections using your search terms. You can also use your search terms to execute electronic word-searches if you are looking at the Restatements on-line. Remember that if you are researching in print and are looking for cases in the appendices, you will need to check multiple volumes, each of which covers a different time period.

The Restatements are useful for obtaining background information about an area of law and the ongoing developments in that area. They also contain, in the appendices, a treasure trove of case annotations. These are helpful for locating controlling cases where the jurisdiction you are interested in has followed the Restatement on a particular point of law. In those situations, you can also use cases from other jurisdictions that have followed the same Restatement rule as persuasive authorities in the controlling jurisdiction. (For more in using out-of-state cases as persuasive authorities, *see* Chapter 7, section G.)

Furthermore, a Restatement rule can itself serve as a persuasive authority in certain situations. Because they contain detailed analysis and are compiled by groups of highly respected lawyers, judges, and professors, the Restatements carry significant weight with the courts. Sometimes, in fact, state courts "adopt" sections of a Restatement, making those sections essentially the law of the state, and giving related sections, as well as the explanatory comments, significant persuasive authority. And even if the courts in a particular jurisdiction have not formally adopted a portion of a Restatement, they still tend to give the Restatements significant deference when the jurisdiction's case law is unclear. Thus, if you are researching an area of law that is principally governed by decisional law, it is always good to see what the Restatements have to say on the subject.

F. OTHER SECONDARY SOURCES

Various other secondary sources, in addition to those discussed above, may at times prove useful to your research. In matters of statutory interpretation, *attorney-general opinions* make good persuasive authorities because courts tend to give them significant deference in determining how statutes should be construed. This is true both at the state and federal levels. You can find attorney-general opinions on Westlaw and Lexis, or at the individual attorneys' general websites. *Uniform acts* and *model codes*, such as the Model Penal Code, are also good persuasive authorities in areas of the law governed primarily by statute. They influence areas of law governed by statute the same way the Restatements influence the common law. Thus, if a certain state has adopted all or part of a model code, you can use case law from other jurisdictions that have adopted the model code as persuasive authority in construing the meaning of similar statutory language.

Another secondary source that can sometimes be useful in researching statutory law is a publication called *Words and Phrases,* which is published by West. Words and Phrases can provide helpful references to cases that construe certain legal terms. More precisely, it catalogues in alphabetical order the headnotes from various cases in which the courts have interpreted key legal terms. It is a helpful tool if you have a legal dispute that turns primarily upon the meaning of a term or concept, as in the case of a statute that contains an ambiguous term.

If you are working in a specialized area of the law, particularly one that is controlled by a complex federal statutory and regulatory scheme (e.g., tax law, workers' compensation, ERISA, securities regulation), *loose-leaf services* (also known as subject-matter services) are a very useful tool. These multi-volume publications, which were traditionally published on 3–ring binders (hence the name), gather in one place a variety of materials—including statutes, regulations, legislative history, cases, commentary, and news of current events—that pertain to a particular specialty. They are updated regularly (e.g., weekly, bi-weekly, or monthly) with replacement pages that keep the subscriber abreast of recent developments in the law. Some of these services are also now available on Westlaw and Lexis; most are available on-line on a subscription basis. By collecting all sorts of relevant materials in one set of volumes, loose-leaf services make the research process much easier when you are working in a specialized area. In fact, for many practitioners who specialize in a fairly narrow area of the law, they are indispensible research aids. (For more on loose-leaf services, *see* Chapter 6, section F.)

Specialized *legal newsletters* are a related type of secondary source. Published on a daily or weekly basis, they keep practitioners abreast of current developments in specialized areas of law, such as banking law or health-care law. Lexis and Westlaw carry a number of these newsletters. If you cannot find what you are looking for there, see if your library has a publication called *Legal Newsletters in Print*, which is a comprehensive guide to specialized legal newsletters.

On the other end of the research spectrum, *Hornbooks* and *Nutshells* can be helpful if you just need some quick background on a general legal topic. These books are similar to treatises, but they are more basic and are primarily intended as study aids for law students.

You should also keep in mind the value of using other lawyers' work product when you research an area of law. Traditionally, many law firms maintained "brief banks" (containing hard copies of actual briefs, motions, and memoranda the firm's attorneys had prepared on various topics), as well as "forms files" (containing samples of various transactional documents their attorneys had created) to assist junior lawyers in preparing their work product. These days, it is usually pretty easy to find such documents on your employer's computer system with a quick word search, even if your employer does not maintain a formal brief bank or form file. Additionally, Westlaw and Lexis have extensive collections of these materials, which, if you find something on point, can give you a head start on your research and also serve as a check on whether your research is on track.

Sample briefs and motions, for example, can be quite useful for litigation research because they provide citations to the authorities that govern a specific issue of law, and they also provide an analysis of the law. But remember that you still need to do your own research, even if you find a brief or motion on point. No two factual scenarios are exactly the same, so you cannot just adopt the analysis of a sample brief and apply it uncritically to your own research problem. You should use these materials as you would any other secondary source: to obtain background information and to give you a head start on your search for primary authorities. Keep in mind, however, that, depending on who wrote them, briefs and memoranda may not be as dependable as traditional secondary sources in describing the law. And in the case of briefs, their analysis will generally not be objective, but will instead be spun in a manner favorable to a particular client's position. Nevertheless, as long as you take heed of these caveats, sample briefs and memoranda can make very helpful research tools.

There are other miscellaneous secondary sources besides those discussed above that you may occasionally want to consult when you set about solving a research problem. Legal newspapers, law-firm websites, government directories, jury instructions, advisory opinions, 50–state surveys: these are just some of the other types of materials that you may find useful in the practice of law from time to time. If you have a difficult research problem and you are unsure what secondary sources are out there, a reference librarian can provide invaluable assistance.

G. DIGESTS AND CITATORS

Strictly speaking, digests and case citators are *finding tools* rather than secondary sources because they do not contain commentary on the law. But like secondary sources, they are useful aids for finding primary authorities. They are also important tools for expanding and updating your case research, as discussed in Chapter 4 above.

1. Digests

Digests are basically collections of short case abstracts, or "annotations," that are arranged alphabetically by subject matter. While they are mainly useful as finding tools, you can also learn a fair amount about an area of law by simply scanning the annotations on a given topic in the appropriate digest. West publishes a digest for each individual state, as well as *regional digests* that compile state-court decisions by area of the country. It also publishes *West's Federal Practice Digest* for federal cases, and a combined digest of all state and federal cases called *West's General Digest*. (Note that the General Digest is non-cumulative, so in order to find earlier cases, you will need to supplement it with *West's Decennial Digests,* which summarize cases by 10–year periods.)

Once considered the "gold standard" for case research, digests remain a viable alternative to on-line electronic word-searches for locating cases, particularly if you do not have access to Westlaw, Lexis, or another on-line subscription service. While digests *per se* are found only in print form, both Westlaw and Lexis have on-line digest functionality that allows you to search for cases by topic. You can access these on-line digest functions by clicking the *Key Numbers* tab at the top of the main page on Westlaw, or by clicking *Search by Topic or Headnote* at the top of the main page on Lexis.

There are advantages and disadvantages to using a digest rather than electronic word-searches to find cases. And often the choice comes down to a matter of personal preference. For important or difficult research, however, I recommend that you search for cases both ways in order to maximize your chances of finding everything on point.

To find cases in the print version of a digest, it is generally easiest to use the topical index. The topical indexes in the West digest system are called *Descriptive Word Indexes*. An alternative method is to search the general outline of the 400 + major topics alphabetically for your general topic, then to look under that broad topic to find your precise topic. If you are not familiar with the subject matter, though, this may be less efficient than using the Descriptive Word Index. To access the Descriptive Word Index, start with the search terms that you generated under **Step 1**. But remember that you may have to modify your search terms to encompass broader or narrower concepts if you do not find what you are looking for with your initial search terms. (For more on modifying your search terms, *see* Chapter 1, section B(1).)

A unique and important feature of West's digest system is the West *Key Number System*. West organizes the law alphabetically into more than 400 major topics, and these are then divided into more and more specific sub-topics until the sub-topics are reduced to individual points of law, each of which is assigned its own unique "key number." There are over 100,000 key numbers, and these key numbers correspond to the points of law found in the headnotes of individual cases. (Key numbers are easily identified by the little symbol of a key next to the topic and number.)

One of the principal benefits of the key-number system is that once you have a case on point, you can use the key number corresponding to that point of law to find other cases on point, either within the same jurisdiction or in other jurisdictions. Suppose, for example, that during your review of secondary sources on contract illegality under New York law, you found a North Carolina case that is right on point for your research project. By using the key number that corresponds to that point of law in the headnotes of the North Carolina case, you can easily find New York cases on the same issue (if there are any) by just looking up that key number in the New York Digest. If you are researching on Westlaw, this is even easier because you just click on the key number you are interested in and then select the appropriate jurisdiction from a list. And while only Westlaw allows you to access its key-number system *per se*, Lexis has a similar capability under its *Search by Topic or Headnote* feature that allows you to do a headnote search to find cases on the same topic as a designated headnote. (For more on using key numbers to expand your case research generally, *see* Chapter 4, section B; for more on using them to find persuasive cases, *see* Chapter 7, section G(3).)

You can also search for cases by *topic* on Westlaw and Lexis if you don't already have a case on point. To access the on-line digest function on Westlaw, you first click on the *Key Numbers* tab at the top of the main page. You then have two options as to how the information is formatted. One allows you to peruse the general outline of the 400+ major topics by clicking on the *Key*

Number Digest Outline link. You can then choose from among the list of broad topics and "drill down" through a series of progressively narrower sub-topics until you find (hopefully) the precise point of law you are looking for. The other option is to search for cases using a broader list of some 47 more conventional topics by clicking on the *KeySearch* link. This latter option is similar to Lexis' digest feature. To search by topic on Lexis, you just click the *Search* tab at the top of the main Lexis page, followed by the *by Topic or Headnote* tab, then choose your topic and sub-topic. Both Westlaw and Lexis allow you to customize your searches by adding your own descriptive search terms to narrow the scope of the existing categories.

If you are researching a digest in print form, remember that you will need to check the supplements and pocket parts in order to find the most recent annotations on the designated topic.

2. Citators

The other important finding tool you will need is the *citator*. The two basic purposes of a citator are: (1) to inform you whether a particular case, statute or regulation has been repealed, overruled, etc., and (2) to find, for a given case, statute, or regulation, all of the cases that have cited that authority. The first function, as discussed in Chapter 6, section J, is vital for making sure your authorities are still valid, and the second function, as discussed in Chapter 4, section C, is important for expanding and updating your research.

The original citator service was *Shepard's*; it is now owned by Lexis and is available on-line as well as in print. Westlaw has a similar on-line product called *KeyCite*. Case citators are significantly more convenient to use on-line than in print, and since the on-line use is not very expensive, few researchers rely on the print versions anymore. To use a citator on-line, you simply type a citation (volume and first page number) into the KeyCite or Shepard's box on the home page and click "go." You can then choose to look at either the citing history for the authority to see if it is still *valid*, or you can look at the broader list of citing references in order to *expand* and *update* your research.

Using a citator to *validate* your research is easy. You just type the citation you want to check into a box and then click the *Citing History* link if you are using KeyCite, or *Shepard's for Validation* if you are using Shepard's. You can then examine any negative history to see whether the authority is still valid. In addition, both services put a red symbol (a flag for Westlaw and a stop sign for Lexis) next to a case to indicate it is no longer valid, at least in part. A red flag or stop sign next to a statute or regulation indicates that it has been amended, repealed, or invalidated. The services put a yellow symbol (a flag for KeyCite, a triangle for Shepard's) next to a case citation to indicate that there is some "negative treatment" (e.g., criticism from the court of another state addressing the same issue), even though the case has not been invalidated. A yellow flag or triangle next to a statute or regulation indicates that it has been re-numbered, limited in its application, or criticized, though not invalidated.

Before you turn in any work product you should always use a citator to validate all of the authorities you rely on (i.e., "Shepardize" your authorities), in order to make sure that your analysis does not depend on an authority that is no longer good law (*see* Chapter 6, section J). Also, if the cases reflecting negative treatment are from the controlling jurisdiction or a superior court, it is a good idea to review the cases yourself, rather than just relying on the citator's editorial staff, to make sure you agree with the citator's assessment.

The other important purpose of citators is to *expand* and *update* your case research. To access this function, you just click on the *Citing References* link if you are using KeyCite, and click *Shepard's for Research* if you are using Shepard's. The only part that is at all tricky is interpreting the symbols the citators use to provide information about the cases they cite. If you go to the KeyCite or Shepard's main on-line pages, however, there are legends that tell you exactly what the various symbols mean. Savvy use of this information can save you significant time in doing your follow-up research. The symbols tell you, for example, whether a citing case has followed, criticized or distinguished the subject case, whether the citing case merely references the subject case or provides a more detailed analysis of the holding, whether the citing case quotes the cited case, etc. Both citators also list headnote numbers next to certain citing cases to let you know that a citing case discusses the same point of law that the case you entered discusses in the designated headnote. (If a citing case does not have a headnote number next to it, you will have to look at the case to determine which headnote(s), if any, it discusses.) Thus, if you are only interested in knowing whether subsequent cases have discussed a point of law summarized by headnote 5 of the *Smith v. Jones* case, you can narrow your review of citing cases to those with the symbol "HN5" next to the citation, which indicates that the citing case discusses the same point of law discussed in headnote 5 of *Smith v. Jones*. As discussed further in Chapter 4, section C, this use of a citator is one of the most powerful tools available to the legal researcher for expanding and updating her research.

Chapter 9

PRIMARY SOURCES OF LAW

Different types of legal documents carry, to varying degrees, the force of law. From municipal ordinances to the U.S. Constitution, lawyers rely on a variety of primary authorities to both analyze what the controlling law is and to persuade those vested with decision-making authority. This chapter discusses the principal types of primary authorities you are likely to rely on in solving legal research problems.

A. CONSTITUTIONS

Constitutions are the foundational documents of a legal system. In the United States, the U.S. Constitution is the highest legal authority in the land, though each state has its own constitution to govern fundamental matters of state law. Constitutions are generally published within statutory compilations; a copy of the U.S. Constitution, for example, can be found in one of the volumes of the United States Code.

It is not likely that you will spend a lot of time on constitutional research in your practice, unless you happen to find yourself in a specialized field, such as media law or federal appellate litigation. In that event, you will probably come to rely heavily on specialized secondary materials, such as loose-leaf services and specialized practice manuals (*see* Chapter 8, sections B and F) to aid your research. But for the general researcher who only occasionally encounters a constitutional issue, constitutional-law research is largely a matter of case-law research, since the courts are charged with interpreting constitutional provisions, and most constitutional provisions, particularly at the federal level, have already been interpreted by the courts. (Don't ignore secondary sources, however; these are very helpful in constitutional research, both for background information and for finding cases.)

If you are called upon to research a constitutional provision as part of a research project, probably the most efficient way to start your search for interpretive authorities is to review the case annotations for that provision in the annotated code where the constitution is published. First, of course, you would look for *controlling* cases on point. (With respect to the United States Constitution, that means cases from the Supreme Court and cases from the controlling circuit; with respect to state constitutions, it means appellate-court cases from the controlling state.) If you can't find any of those, then you would likely search for *persuasive cases*. If you are looking for persuasive cases interpreting the *U.S. Constitution*, you would normally look to district-court decisions and to appellate cases from the other circuits. You might also look to state-supreme-court cases that interpret the U.S. Constitution. If you are looking for persuasive cases to interpret a *state constitution*, and the operative language from that constitution tracks the U.S. Constitution, you can look to federal cases interpreting the equivalent provision in the U.S. Constitution for guidance. You could also look to decisions from other states for guidance, if they construe similar language in their own constitutions, or to trial-court cases from the controlling state, if they are published. (For more on using non-controlling cases as persuasive authorities, *see* Chapter 7, section G.)

In some circumstances—where, for example, you can't even find any persuasive cases on point—you might want to research historical materials to interpret a constitutional provision. In interpreting a provision in the U.S. Constitution, for instance, you could look at historical records of the proceedings at the Constitutional Convention, or at the records of the subsequent state-ratification debates. You should talk with your supervisor before undertaking this type of historical research, but if you do decide to proceed with it, there are some good compilations available regarding the history of the U.S. Constitution that will aid your research efforts. Your reference librarian can help you locate them.

B. STATUTES

Statutes are the product of legislation. When a statute is first enacted by a legislature, it is published on its own as a *slip law*. It is subsequently compiled with the other statutes that the legislature has enacted in a particular legislative session, and together these are published as *session laws*. These session laws are then incorporated into the jurisdiction's *statutory code,* which contains all the statutes currently in force in that jurisdiction. If you have an issue of federal law, statutes are codified in the United States

Code; if you have an issue of state law, statutes are codified in the applicable state code.

In most jurisdictions, the session laws constitute the official version of the legislation in the event there is any discrepancy between these various publications. The codes, however, being organized by subject matter, are much more accessible for purposes of research. Accordingly, most lawyers use the annotated versions of codes (e.g., the *United States Code Annotated* or the *United States Code Service*) for their research, since these are updated more frequently than non-annotated versions and also contain short summaries of the cases interpreting the statutes.

Statutory interpretation frequently forms the centerpiece of a legal research problem. As long as a legislative enactment is not unconstitutional, it trumps other sources of law. Thus, except in those relatively rare circumstances when a court is called upon to determine the constitutionality of a statute, it is the court's job merely to interpret and apply the statute.

Case law does dominate certain areas of state law, such as torts and contracts, where legislatures have traditionally deferred to the common-law tradition. Accordingly, if you are researching a problem in one of these areas, there may not be a statute on point. But even in these areas of law traditionally left to the courts, legislatures in recent decades have shown an increasing willingness to become involved. So it is always a good idea to check whether there are any relevant statutes that might affect your legal analysis if you are uncertain whether decisional law controls. (*See* Chapter 3, section C(1) for a discussion of how to determine whether an area of law is controlled by legislation, and if so, how to go about finding the relevant statute(s).)

Once you locate a statute on point, you will then need to expand and update your statutory research. First, you should *expand* your research by checking whether there are any related statutory provisions that might affect your analysis. To do this, you should review the sections preceding and following the relevant statutory section to see if they are also on point. Then you should look at the *topical index* to see if there are other statutory sections listed under the relevant topic, and whether there are any related topics listed in the index. (It is also a good idea to check the code's table of contents to see whether any other sections of the code look like they might apply.) And finally, in order to ensure that you haven't missed any relevant provision, you may want to run an electronic word-search of the entire code, using key terms from the relevant statute (e.g., from the statute's definition section) as your search terms.

The next step is to *update* your research. If you are researching in print, you should start by reviewing the relevant pocket parts and supplements to see whether the statutory language has been modified. Then check the editorial notes at the end of the statute. These will give you, among other things, the dates of any significant amendments, along with references to the relevant slip laws and session laws. This information is important if you need to determine whether your particular research problem is governed by the current statutory language or some earlier version of the statute, and also whether a given case interpreting the statute is still valid or has been superseded by a change in the statutory language. (*See* Chapter 3, section C(1), for more on researching an earlier version of a statute.)

Next you should use a citator (Shepard's or KeyCite) to make sure that the statute has not been recently modified or repealed by the legislature, or stricken by a reviewing court. (*See* Chapter 8, section G(2) for more on using citators.) The citator will also provide you references to the most recent cases, which may not have been published yet in the annotated codes.

If you are researching on-line with a commercial service such as Westlaw or Lexis, any recent changes to the statutory language will automatically be reflected, since these services are updated continually. But if you are researching in print, you will need to look at the jurisdiction's *session laws* if the citator indicates that there are very recent changes to the statutory language that are not reflected in the pocket parts and supplements to the code volumes. (Similarly, if you are researching in print sources and you are trying to locate a very recent statute, you may need to check the session laws, since statutes are published as session laws before they are codified.) At the federal level, the session laws are published as the *United States Statutes at Large,* which can be found in various sources, including the *United States Code Congressional and Administrative News, HeinOnline,* and the United States government's free *GPO Access* site (www.gpoaccess. gov), as well as on commercial services such as Westlaw and Lexis.

After you have expanded and updated your statutory research, you are ready to undertake further research regarding the scope of the legislative scheme and the proper interpretation of the statutory language. This requires you to look at other primary sources, such as administrative regulations, interpretive case law, and perhaps also the statute's legislative history. These sources are discussed in the subsequent sections of this chapter. (For more on using these other primary sources as part of your statutory research, *see* Chapter 3, section C(1).)

C. REGULATIONS

Regulations are rules generated by agencies to implement statutes. At times, Congress or a state legislature will authorize an agency to promulgate regulations in order to provide more complexity to a particular legislative scheme than Congress or the state legislature wants to include in the actual legislation. Congress, for example, has authorized the Internal Revenue Service to generate a detailed regulatory scheme that expands upon the provisions of the U.S. tax code. Essentially, in these situations, the legislative body delegates limited authority to an agency to make law, subject to the ultimate approval of the legislature. Regulations flesh out the scope and applicability of a statute, but they cannot conflict with the statute or exceed the agency's legislative mandate, or else they are subject to being invalidated by the courts.

Federal regulations are codified in the *Code of Federal Regulations* (i.e., the "C.F.R."). However, newly promulgated federal regulations first appear in a government publication called the *Federal* Register. They are later added to the C.F.R. when it is republished every year. Both of these publications are available on Westlaw and Lexis, as well as in print. You can also easily access them on the federal government's free *GPO Access* website (www. gpoaccess.gov).

The manner in which regulations at the state level are compiled varies by state. But most states tend to follow the federal system, publishing their regulations initially in registers similar to the Federal Register, and then codifying them later in administrative codes similar to the C.F.R. If you have access to a commercial service such as Westlaw or Lexis, you can find the regulatory codes and registers for a majority of states, along with some other helpful state-administrative materials. Certain loose-leaf services also contain updated compilations of state regulatory materials pertaining to particular specialties, along with relevant statutes, cases, and secondary sources. Free state-government websites are another good source for obtaining state administrative materials. Normally you can find these websites quite easily with a simple internet search, but if you are having trouble, you can consult the National Association of Secretaries of State's free website (www. administrativerules.org), which lists the relevant websites for all the states that have made their codes and registers available online.

Once you have located and reviewed one or more regulations that relate to your research problem, you will need to *expand* your regulatory research to ensure that you have found all relevant provisions. You should start by reviewing the surrounding sections of the applicable administrative code to see if there are any other regulations that pertain to your subject. Then you should search the administrative code at large for other relevant regulations. The topical index and finding tables for the administrative code are helpful for this, as is the main table of contents at the beginning of the code. Alternatively, you can perform electronic word-searches on Westlaw of Lexis to find other regulations that might relate to your problem, using key terms from the regulatory language (and from the definition section of the regulation, if there is one).

Next, after having expanded your regulatory research, you need to *update* your research to make sure that the relevant regulations have not been amended or repealed since the last publication date. Updating regulations is automatic if you are researching on-line with commercial services such as Lexis or Westlaw, as these services continually update the regulations for you. The government's free *GPO Access* website (www.gpoaccess. gov) also publishes an unofficial version of the C.F.R., called the *e-C.F.R.,* which is updated continuously. And loose-leaf services also update their contents on a regular basis.

But if you are not using one of these services, the updating process is a little more cumbersome. The traditional way to update *federal* regulations is by using a government publication called the *List of C.F.R. Sections Affected (L.S.A.),* which tells you, for any given regulation, whether it has been affected by any later agency action; if so, it directs you to the citation for the relevant Federal Register entry that affects the regulation. The *L.S.A.* is only published monthly, so you will also need to check the *Table of C.F.R Parts Affected,* which is found on the back of the most current issue of the Federal Register, to make sure that the regulation has not changed in the current month. If there have been any recent changes, the *Table of C.F.R. Parts Affected* will refer you to the relevant Federal Register cite(s) so that you can look at the changes.

The *L.S.A.* is available on-line as well as in print. The easiest way to access it is on the government's *GPO Access* website, where it is part of the "Executive Resources" collection. Remember that you can also access the on-line version of the Federal Register (which is published daily) on the *GPO Access* website, as well as the on-line version of the C.F.R.

After you have expanded and updated your regulatory research, you should then check to see whether there are any *cases* that interpret the applicable regulatory language. Case law is important in construing the meaning of regulations, just as it is for statutes. (For more on finding cases that interpret regulations, *see* Chapter 3, section C(2).)

If you are doing in-depth administrative research, you will generally want to look also for any *agency decisions* that might interpret the relevant regulation(s). Agencies have an adjudicative function as well as a rule-making function. Like courts, agencies conduct evidentiary hearings, called *administrative hearings.* These are less formal than court proceedings and are held before administrative law judges who work for the agency, rather than independent judges. While they are not binding like controlling court decisions, agency decisions do nevertheless shed light on how an agency interprets its own regulations. Thus, they can be useful in predicting how an agency is likely to apply a regulation in future cases, and they can also be useful in persuading an agency that it should treat your client the same as a similarly situated party to a reported agency decision.

To locate agency decisions, you can look at the relevant agency's web site, or at a loose-leaf service that focuses on that particular area of administrative law. Alternatively, you can use a citator; KeyCite and Shepard's both provide citations to a limited number of agency decisions. And Westlaw and Lexis both carry a number of agency decisions. On Westlaw, they are listed automatically, along with links to other useful materials, under the *RegulationsPlus* feature.

It can also sometimes be helpful, in construing a vague or ambiguous regulation, to see how courts have interpreted similar language contained in other regulations in the administrative code. If, for example, there is an important, undefined term in a regulation you are dealing with, and there is a court decision that defines the term with respect to another regulation, you can use that decision as persuasive authority for interpreting the language of the regulation that you are interested in. (Likewise, if that term is defined elsewhere in the code with respect to another regulation, you can look to that definition for guidance in interpreting the language of the regulation you are interested in.)

Finally, if you want to do even more in-depth regulatory research, you may want to look at other administrative materials, such as *agency policy statements, agency manuals*, and *advisory letters*, which can shed some light on the agency's own interpretation of the regulation. These types of materials are often published on agency websites. A good number of them are available on Westlaw and Lexis as well. You may also want to look at the history of the rule-making process by examining the proposed rule, the public comments that were generated in response to the proposed rule, and any changes the agency made in response to the public comments. For federal administrative rules, the proposed rule and the public comments are published in the Federal Register and can be located through cross-references found in the final version of the rule that is published in the Federal Register.

D. SOURCES OF LEGISLATIVE HISTORY

Another tool for interpreting statutory language is *legislative history*, which can be used to infer the legislature's intent as to the meaning of a statute, particularly in situations where the language of the statute is unclear and there are no regulations or interpretive cases to guide your research. A statute's legislative history consists principally of its stated purpose, the bills that gave rise to the final legislation, the statements of the bills' sponsors, the reports of the committees that approved the bills, the records of committee hearings, the records of floor debates, and signing statements. Legislative history is not something you need to investigate every time your research problem involves a statute. Most of the time, the plain meaning of the statute, case law, and any regulations promulgated under the statute should be sufficient to guide your analysis. But in the appropriate context legislative history can be an important tool, such as when the meaning or applicability of a statutory provision remains unclear even after you have carefully reviewed the statutory language and any available interpretive cases.

Putting together the legislative history of a statute basically involves gathering all the relevant bills, committee reports, transcripts, and other materials generated as the legislation works it way through the legislative process, then analyzing them to determine whether they shed light on the legislature's intent. You should always discuss with your supervisor whether it is worth pursuing the legislative history of a given statute before you start looking for these materials, since preparing a full legislative history can be fairly time-consuming if you have to start from scratch.

In addition, you should always check whether the materials have already been compiled before you undertake a full legislative history from scratch. Sometimes a case that interprets a statute, for example, will also analyze its legislative history. Even if the holding of the case is not directly relevant to your research, you can use the citations to quickly locate the relevant legislative-history materials. Legislative histories for a number of federal statutes are catalogued in two well-known directories: Bernard D. Reams' *Federal Legislative Histories: An Annotated Bibliography and Index to Officially Published Sources*; and Nancy P. Johnson's *Sources of Compiled Legislative Histories*. These should be available in any sizeable law library. Lexis and Westlaw have also compiled legislative histories on a number of statutes. And many loose-leaf services compile legislative histories for important statutes they discuss. If you are researching in a specialized area such as tax law, for example, you can use the finding tables in a loose-leaf service such as CCH's *Standard Federal Tax Reporter* to find the legislative histories for a number of important provisions in the tax code. And finally, there are certain other commercial services that compile legislative histories; check with your librarian to see if these are available through your library.

If you can't locate a pre-packaged legislative history, and you decide that finding the legislative history for a particular statute is important to your research, then you will have to compile it yourself. For federal statutes, the most accessible source for a legislative-history overview is the *United States Code Congressional and Administrative News* ("U.S.C.C.A.N."). It is published by West and is available on-line as well as in print. U.S.C.C.A.N. does not provide complete legislative histories, but it often provides quite a bit of useful information about a statute, including its committee reports, which are generally considered the most significant of the legislative-history documents. U.S.C.C.A.N. also provides the important identifying numbers and dates for a statute and its earlier bills, which makes it easy to locate additional legislative-history materials.

If you need a more in-depth legislative history than you can obtain through U.S.C.A.N.N., a helpful resource is a publication called the *CIS Index*, which is now available on Lexis as the

LexisNexis Congressional service. The CIS Index provides finding aids and references to a variety of legislative-history materials, including committee reports, committee prints, hearing reports, and the original bills. It also provides references to the *Congressional Record,* which contains the floor debate for each bill.

A number of these documents are readily available on free websites. *Thomas* (www.thomas.gov) is a free website set up by the Library of Congress. *Thomas* contains the texts of bills, committee reports, excerpts from the Congressional Record, and other information related to federal statutes. Another free government website that can be useful is *GPO Access* (www.gpoaccess. gov), which contains many of the same documents, in addition to executive materials. The websites for the U.S. House (www.house. gov) and the U.S. Senate (www.senate.gov) also have links (click on "Legislative Archive" in the House site, "Legislation and Records" in the Senate site) through which you can access various legislative-history resources.

Finally, if you are struggling to put together a legislative history on a statute, don't forget about your friendly law librarian. A good reference librarian will have significant expertise on compiling legislative histories and can be a valuable resource in helping you find the necessary materials.

The above discussion has focused on *federal* legislative history. The documents that are germane to compiling a *state* legislative history are similar to those discussed above, and generally they are compiled in a similar manner. But many states do not publish everything, and even when they do, finding the relevant materials is often more difficult. For that reason alone, it is less common for lawyers and judges to employ a legislative-history analysis in construing a state statute than it is for a federal statute. Still, if you are diligent, legislative histories can often be compiled for state legislation. Your best bet for free research is to try state-government web sites. Another good option is to look in state-specific practice manuals or loose-leaf services. You can also locate the legislative materials and legislative-history materials available for any given state in William H. Manz's *Guide to State Legislation, Legislative History, and Administrative Materials.*

Finally, Westlaw and Lexis have compiled basic legislative-history materials for most states, which can be helpful in getting you started on compiling a state legislative history.

E. CASES

When law students and beginning lawyers think of legal research, they normally have case research in mind. And indeed, case research is at the hub of most legal research projects. In areas of the law that are controlled by a constitution, a statute, or an administrative regulation, judges have the final say in interpreting the meaning of the governing language, so cases are key to construing these other primary sources; and in areas of the law that are not controlled by another primary source, judicial opinions themselves form the law. Thus, it is critical for the legal researcher to be skilled in finding and working with case law.

Judicial decisions are compiled in multi-volume print collections called *reporters*. Different courts publish their decisions in different reporters. United States Supreme Court opinions are published in three main reporters: the *U.S. Reports* (the official reporter), the *Supreme Court Reporter*, published by West, and the *United States Supreme Court Reports, Lawyers' Edition*, published by LexisNexis. Decisions from the United States courts of appeals are published in the *Federal Reporter*. And noteworthy decisions from the United States district courts are published in the *Federal Supplement*. Additional district-court decisions pertaining to federal procedural rules are compiled in the *Federal Rules Decisions*. There are also some lesser-known reporters published by commercial services that compile federal cases dealing with specialized areas of the law.

State-appellate-court decisions (most states do not publish trial-court decisions) are published in both the West Regional Reporter System, and in official state reporters. The West Regional Reporter System divides the country into seven regions and compiles the various state appellate-court decisions for each of those regions (e.g., *North Western Reports, South Eastern Reports*, etc.). The official state reporters, on the other hand, compile state-appellate decisions by court. Colorado Supreme Court cases, for example, are published in the *Colorado Reports*, while Colorado Court of Appeals cases are published in the *Colorado Court of Appeals Reports*. The West regional reporter that covers Colorado (which is the *Pacific Reporter*, oddly enough) compiles cases from both of these courts, along with appellate decisions from Alaska, Hawaii, and all of the western states other than Texas.

The on-line commercial services carry all of the cases found in these reporters, and they generally make them available earlier than the cases become available in print. They also make available a number of cases that are not published in the official reporters, including some state *trial-court* orders. You will need to check a jurisdiction's local rules before citing an unpublished case, however, since some courts limit or prohibit their use.

Many courts also post their decisions on free web sites. These tend not to be updated as frequently as the commercial services, however, and they may not be as complete in their coverage. The web sites also lack the comprehensive search capacity that Westlaw and Lexis offer. The same is true of most free on-line services such as Findlaw and the Legal Information Institute's website. Your best bet for free case research is probably Google Scholar, which is easy to use and has a robust search engine.

Researching case law involves two principal tasks: finding relevant cases, and then expanding and updating one's case research. The former task is discussed at length throughout Chapter 3, section C. The latter task is the subject of Chapter 4.

F. COURT RULES

Court rules include the procedures that govern lawsuits, as well as more substantive rules, such as evidentiary standards and attorney disciplinary rules. At the federal level, the court rules you are most likely to research are the *Federal Rules of Civil Procedure* and the *Federal Rules of Evidence*. You might also be asked to look at the *Federal Rules of Criminal Procedure* or the *Federal Rules of Appellate Procedure*. State courts have similar compilations of court rules, which are often modeled after the federal rules. In addition, individual courts often have their own "local rules" that supplement the state or federal rules. Any time you are litigating before a court, you should familiarize yourself with both the general rules for the jurisdiction and that particular court's local rules.

Finding court rules is easy. One-volume compilations of the principal court rules for any given jurisdiction are published by West and are readily available. Most litigators have their own desk copies of the federal rules and of their individual state's rules. Free on-line access to the federal court rules is available at the *U.S. Courts'* website (www.uscourts.gov); just click on the "Federal Rulemaking" link. This site also has links to all the local rules of the various federal courts. Most state-court systems have similar sites that publish state court rules on-line without charge. If you run an internet search for "court rules," you can generally locate the sites easily. Most have addresses similar to the *U.S. Courts'* website: Michigan's state-court website, for example is located at www.courts.michigan.gov; Texas' site is located at www. courts.state.tx.us; California's site is located at www.courtinfo.ca. gov, and so forth. In addition, Westlaw, Lexis and the other on-line providers carry court rules for every jurisdiction.

Like constitutions, statutes and regulations, court rules are subject to interpretation by the courts. Thus, if you have a research problem involving the meaning of a particular court rule (e.g., whether a party opposing a motion for summary judgment under Rule 56 has raised sufficient evidence to defeat the motion for summary judgment), you will want to search for interpretive cases, starting with cases from the controlling jurisdiction. You can use the annotated version of the court rules for that jurisdiction to view summaries of cases interpreting the relevant rule; generally these annotated versions of court rules can be found within the jurisdiction's annotated statutory code. Cases interpreting court rules can also be located by using a case citator (*see* Chapter 8, section G(2)). Just type the citation for the relevant court rule into Shepard's or KeyCite, just as you would for a statute, a case, or a regulation, and the citator will provide citations to all the cases that have cited that court rule. You can also run an electronic word-search in Westlaw or Lexis to find cases that interpret a particular court rule, using the citation for the rule as one of your search terms.

Keep in mind that if a state's court rules track the federal rules, as is often the case, you can use federal cases interpreting a particular federal rule as persuasive authority for interpreting a parallel state rule. This can be very helpful when you cannot find any state cases on point. (For more on using persuasive authorities, *see* Chapter 7, section G.) Remember also to review the Advisory Notes and Amendments at the end of the annotated rule you are researching, as these too can shed light on the meaning of a rule.

Certain secondary sources are valuable for researching court rules as well. For example, there are two large multi-volume treatises on the federal rules that are well-respected: Wright & Miller's *Federal Practice & Procedure*, and *Moore's Federal Practice*. These treatises are often cited by the courts, so they can be quite useful as persuasive authorities in the appropriate case. In addition, many states have practice manuals devoted to their individual court rules. These are helpful when a state's rules do not track the federal rules.

G. OTHER PRIMARY AUTHORITIES

In addition to the sources discussed above, you may from time to time need to consult more obscure primary sources to find the answer to a legal research problem. For example, if you are researching an issue such as a zoning restriction, your answer will likely depend upon *local law*. Usually municipalities have *charters* that set out their basic organizational laws, as well as *ordinances* and *regulations* that are compiled into municipal codes. They are often available on-line at the county's or municipality's website. You should be able to find the relevant website with a simple Google or Yahoo search. Otherwise, a directory of local governmental websites is available at a free website called *State and Local Government on the Net* (www.statelocalgov.net). Westlaw and Lexis also make a number of local laws available on-line. You can also contact the local municipal or county clerk's office directly if you are having a hard time locating local laws, or if you want to make sure that you have the latest version of the laws. (*See* Chapter 3, section C(4), for additional information on researching local law.)

At the other end of the research spectrum, you may some-times need to address an issue of *international law*. Most com-monly, this involves looking at one or more treaties between the United States and other countries, and perhaps also at the deci-sional law of an international tribunal, such as the International Court of Justice. International research is a complicated subject, but you can find a basic index of all U.S. treaties in a State Department publication called *Treaties in Force*, which is available for free on the U.S. State Department's website (www.state.gov). You can also obtain a wealth of free information about treaties on the United Nations' website (www.un.org). Look for the "Trea-ties" link on the International Law page. Lexis and Westlaw also have collections of materials relating to international law, includ-ing a number of important treaties.

Indian law (also known as *Tribal law* or *Native–American law*) is another specialized source of primary authority. While much of this law derives from federal statutes, regulations and case law, the individual sovereign tribes have their own legal systems as well, including their own constitutions, codes and decisional law. A lot of this material is available for free on the internet, though you may have to dig for it a bit. The websites of certain law school libraries also have collections devoted to Native American legal resources, such as the *Native American Legal Resource Site* (www.law.ou.edu/native), which is available on the University of Oklahoma College of Law's website. Similarly, the Tribal Law and Policy Institute has a helpful website called the *Tribal Court Clearinghouse* (www.tribal-institute.org), which can direct you to relevant primary authorities and other useful mate-rials. And Westlaw and Lexis also carry fairly extensive collections of materials pertaining to Indian law.

One other primary source that deserves mention here is the *executive order*. U.S. Presidents have long relied upon their inher-ent executive power to issue executive orders and proclamations (perhaps the most famous of which is the Emancipation Proclama-tion) in order to facilitate the administration of the executive branch. Governors of states have similar authority, though it tends to be more limited than presidential authority. Should you need to research an executive order or proclamation, federal executive orders are published first in the Federal Register and then in the C.F.R., in the same way administrative regulations are published (*see* section C of this chapter). In addition, U.S.C.A.N.N. includes important executive orders, along with legislative-history materials (*see* section D of this chapter). You can also access an extensive collection of presidential executive orders, along with many other useful presidential documents, at the American Presidency Project's free on-line website (www.presidency.ucsb.edu); just click on the "Documents" link. As for state executive orders, you can generally access these on free state-government websites—often at the website for the governor's office. Westlaw and Lexis carry executive orders as well, both presidential and gubernatorial.

As always, if you are having difficulty finding an obscure primary source, you should seek out the advice of a reference librarian. Reference librarians are a valuable resource, and they are there to help you.

INDEX

References are to Pages

143